NORTHSTAR

LISTENING AND SPEAKING

Basic/Low Intermediate

SECOND EDITION

Robin Mills
Laurie Frazier

Series Editors
Frances Boyd
Carol Numrich

NorthStar: Listening and Speaking, Basic/Low Intermediate
Second Edition

Pearson Education, 10 Bank Street, White Plains, NY 10606

Pronunciation consultant: Linda Lane
Development director: Penny Laporte
Project manager: Debbie Sistino
Senior development editor: Françoise Leffler
Vice president, director of design and production: Rhea Banker
Executive managing editor: Linda Moser
Production editor: Marc Oliver
Production coordinator: Melissa Leyva
Director of manufacturing: Patrice Fraccio
Senior manufacturing buyer: Dave Dickey
Photo research: Aerin Csigay
Cover design: Rhea Banker
Cover art: Detail of Wandbild aus dem Tempel der Sehnsucht\dorthin/, 1922,
    30 Mural from the temple of desire\there/ 26.7 × 37.5 cm; oil transfer
    drawing and water color on plaster-primed gauze; The Metropolitan
    Museum of Art, N.Y. The Berggruen Klee Collection, 1984. (1984.315.33)
    Photograph © 1986 The Metropolitan Museum of Art.
    © 2003 Artists Rights Society (ARS), New York / VG Bild-Kunst, Bonn
Text design: Quorum Creative Services
Text composition: ElectraGraphics, Inc.
Text font: 11/13 Sabon
Illustration credits: see p. 187
Photo credits: see p. 187

Wandbild aus dem Tempel
der Sehnsucht ↖ dorthin ↗
Paul Klee

Library of Congress Cataloging-in-Publication Data

Frazier, Laurie Leach.
    NorthStar. Listening and speaking, basic/low intermediate / Laurie
Frazier, Robin Mills.
        p. cm.
    Includes index.
    1. English language—Textbooks for foreign speakers. 2. English
language—Spoken English—Problems, exercises, etc. 3. Listening—
Problems, exercises, etc. I. Title: Listening and speaking, basic/low
intermediate. II. Mills, Robin III. Title.

PE1128.F6749 2003
428.2'4—dc21

                                                              2003047518

ISBN: 0-201-75568-8 (Student Book)
       0-13-143912-X (Student Book with CD)

Printed in the United States of America
5 6 7 8 9 10—CRK—09 08 07 06 05
3 4 5 6 7 8 9 10—CRK—09 08 07 06 05 04

Contents

Welcome to NORTHSTAR

Second Edition

NorthStar leads the way in integrated skills series. The Second Edition remains an innovative, five-level series written for students with academic as well as personal language goals. Each unit of the thematically linked Reading and Writing strand and Listening and Speaking strand explores intellectually challenging, contemporary themes to stimulate critical thinking skills while building language competence.

Four easy to follow sections—Focus on the Topic, Focus on Reading/Focus on Listening, Focus on Vocabulary, and Focus on Writing/Focus on Speaking—invite students to focus on the process of learning through **NorthStar**.

Thematically Based Units

NorthStar engages students by organizing language study thematically. Themes provide stimulating topics for reading, writing, listening, and speaking.

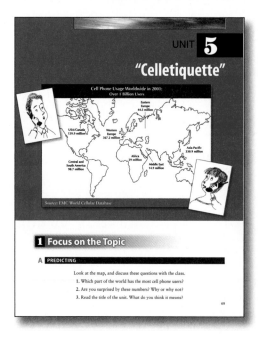

Extensive Support to Build Skills for Academic Success

Creative activities help students develop language-learning strategies, such as predicting and identifying main ideas and details.

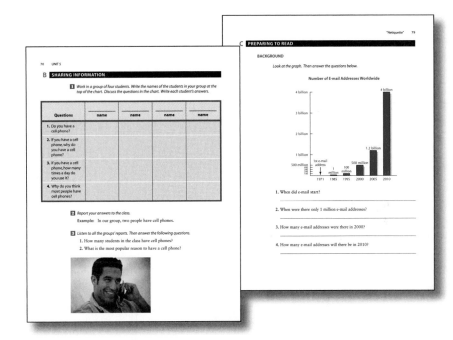

High-Interest Listening and Reading Selections

The two listening or reading selections in each unit present contrasting viewpoints to enrich students' understanding of the content while building language skills.

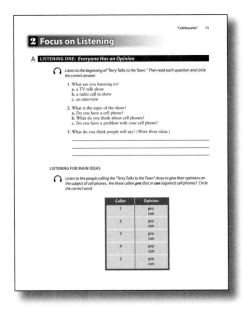

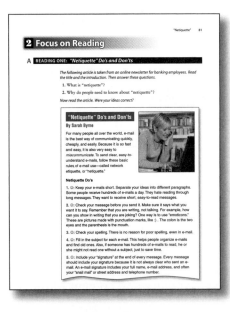

Critical Thinking Skill Development

Critical thinking skills, such as synthesizing information or reacting to the different viewpoints in the two reading or listening selections, are practiced throughout each unit, making language learning meaningful.

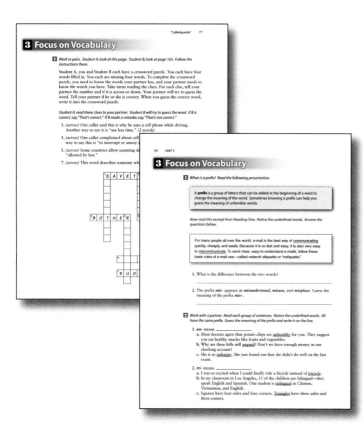

Extensive Vocabulary Practice

Students are introduced to key, contextualized vocabulary to help them comprehend the listening and reading selections. They also learn idioms, collocations, and word forms to help them explore, review, play with, and expand their spoken and written expression.

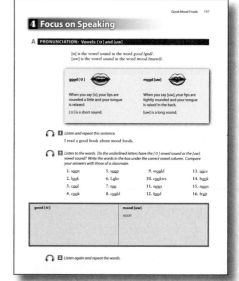

Powerful Pronunciation Practice

A carefully designed pronunciation syllabus in the Listening and Speaking strand focuses on topics such as stress, rhythm, and intonation. Theme-based pronunciation practice reinforces the vocabulary and content of the unit.

Content-Rich Grammar Practice

Each thematic unit integrates the study of grammar with related vocabulary and cultural information. The grammatical structures are drawn from the listening or reading selections and offer an opportunity for students to develop accuracy in speaking or writing about the topic.

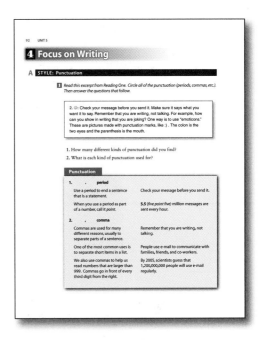

Extensive Opportunity for Discussion and Writing

Challenging and imaginative speaking activities, writing topics, and research assignments allow students to apply the language, grammar, style, and content they've learned.

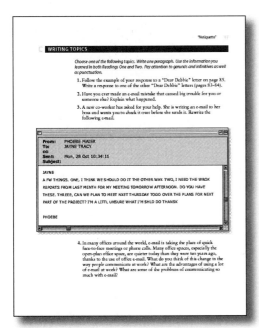

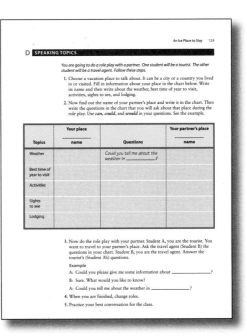

Writing Activity Book

The companion *Writing Activity Book* leads students through the writing process with engaging writing assignments. Skills and vocabulary from **NorthStar: Reading and Writing,** are reviewed and expanded as students learn the process of prewriting, organizing, revising, and editing.

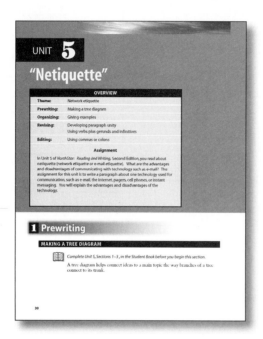

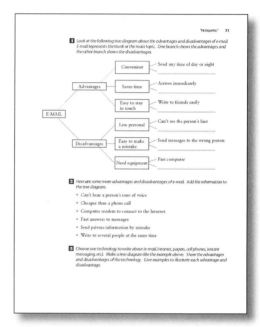

Audio Program

All the pronunciation, listening, and reading selections have been professionally recorded. The audio program includes audio CDs as well as audio cassettes.

Teacher's Manual with Achievement Tests

Each book in the series has an accompanying *Teacher's Manual* with step-by-step teaching suggestions, time guidelines, and expansion activities. Also included in each *Teacher's Manual* are reproducible unit-by-unit tests. The Listening and Speaking strand tests are recorded on CD and included in the *Teacher's Manual*. Packaged with each *Teacher's Manual* for the Reading and Writing strand is a TestGen CD-ROM that allows teachers to create and customize their own **NorthStar** tests. Answer Keys to both the Student Book and the Tests are included, along with a unit-by-unit word list of key vocabulary.

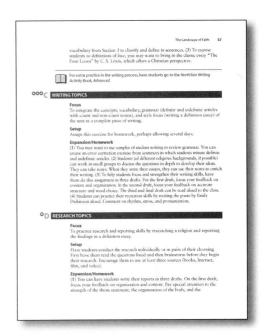

NorthStar Video Series

Engaging, authentic video clips, including cartoons, documentaries, interviews, and biographies correlate to the themes in **NorthStar.** There are four videos, one for each level of **NorthStar**, Second edition, containing 3- to 5- minute segments for each unit. Worksheets for the video can be found on the **NorthStar** Companion Website.

Companion Website

http://www.longman.com/northstar includes resources for students and teachers such as additional vocabulary activities, Web-based links and research, video worksheets, and correlations to state standards.

Scope and Sequence

Unit	Critical Thinking Skills	Listening Tasks
1 **Offbeat Jobs** Theme: Work Listening One: *What's My Job?* 　A game show Listening Two: *More Offbeat Jobs* 　A report on an unusual website	Classify information Rank personal values and preferences in work Relate personal skills to job responsibilities Infer word meaning from context Infer situational context Support opinions with information from the interviews Assess a person's character and recommend a job	Listen and predict Listen for main ideas Listen for details Interpret speaker's tone and attitude Sort information from the interview Relate listenings to personal experience Synthesize information from both listenings
2 **A Piece of the Country in the City** Theme: The Country and the City Listening One: *Community Gardens* 　A radio interview Listening Two: *Let's Hear from Our Listeners* 　A radio call-in show	Classify information Compare and contrast city and country life Interpret a graph Infer word meaning from context Infer situational context Categorize sounds	Listen and predict Listen and identify main ideas Listen for details Interpret speaker's tone and attitude Relate listenings to own community Summarize information from the two listenings Listen to and take notes on student reports
3 **A Penny Saved Is a Penny Earned** Theme: Money Listening One: *A Barter Network* 　A community meeting Listening Two: *Saving Money* 　Three conversations	Interpret a cartoon Assess personal consumer habits Interpret a time-line on the history of money Compare and contrast money and bartering systems Infer word meaning from context Identify advantages and disadvantages Evaluate consumer behavior	Listen and predict Listen for main ideas Listen and take notes on details using an outline Interpret speaker's tone and emotions Relate listening to personal experiences Listen and take notes using a chart Summarize information from the two listenings Listen to and take notes on student reports
4 **At Your Service: Service Animals** Theme: Animals Listening One: *Kimba, the Hero Dog* 　A news report Listening Two: *Do People Help Animals Too?* 　A conversation	Interpret a bar graph Compare knowledge of service animals Infer word meaning from context Compare classmates' attitudes toward pets Interpret points of view Compare values about pets across cultures Evaluate appropriate language usage	Listen and predict Listen and identify main ideas Listen for details Interpret speaker's tone and attitude Relate listening to personal values Listen to and comment on student reports

Speaking Tasks	Pronunciation	Vocabulary	Grammar
Make predictions Express and defend opinions Act out a conversation Make small talk Interview a classmate Brainstorm offbeat jobs Report research findings	Stress patterns of nouns and adjectives	Context clues Dictionary work Word definitions	Descriptive adjectives
Make predictions Share opinions Role-play Express agreement with *too* and *not either* Make past tense statements Act out a scripted conversation and news report Talk about favorite places Report observations on local urban greening	Regular verbs in the simple past tense	Context clues Word definitions	Simple past tense
Make predictions Share opinions and experiences Role-play a group negotiation Make suggestions and come to an agreement Compare products Act out scripted conversations Ask and answer questions Simulate bartering Report on comparison shopping research	Numbers and prices	Context clues Word definitions	Comparative adjectives
Make predictions Survey classmates Express opinions Construct and perform a dialogue Ask for more information Ask and answer information questions Conduct an interview Report interview results	Intonation of *wh-* questions	Context clues Word definitions Synonyms Appropriate word usage	Simple present tense— *wh-* questions with *do*

Unit	Critical Thinking Skills	Listening Tasks
5 **"Celletiquette"** Theme: Cell Phone Etiquette Listening One: *Everyone Has an Opinion* A radio call-in show Listening Two: *Our Listeners Write* A radio call-in show	Interpret a map and graphs Identify rationales for cell phone use Summarize and analyze student responses Infer information not explicit in text Infer word meaning from context Classify information Propose solutions Hypothesize reasons for cell phone behavior	Listen and predict Listen and identify speakers' opinions Listen for supporting details Interpret speaker's tone and attitude Relate listening to personal etiquette standards Synthesize information from both listenings Listen to and comment on role-plays Listen to and take notes on students' reports
6 **Is It Women's Work?** Theme: Male and Female Roles Listening One: *Who's Taking Care of the Children?* A TV talk show Listening Two: *Who Is Right for the Job?* Three conversations	Identify assumptions about family roles Interpret a graph and a chart Identify personal assumptions Infer word meaning from context Rank child-care solutions Support opinions with reasoning Compare gender roles across cultures	Listen and predict Listen and identify chronology in a text Listen for details Interpret speaker's tone and attitude Listen and take notes using a chart Relate listenings to personal values Synthesize information from both listenings Listen to and comment on student reports
7 **Good-Mood Foods** Theme: Food Listening One: *Would You Like to Be on the Radio?* A radio show Listening Two: *What's the Matter?* Four cases	Identify personal attitudes toward food Interpret a chart Infer word meaning from context Categorize words and sounds Propose solutions Compare and contrast sounds Rank student findings	Listen and predict Listen for main ideas Listen and identify details Interpret speaker's tone and reaction Relate listening to personal experiences Listen and take notes using a chart Integrate information from both listenings in discussion Listen to and comment on student reports and reviews

Speaking Tasks	**Pronunciation**	**Vocabulary**	**Grammar**
Make predictions Survey classmates Share opinions Compare and discuss solutions Use new vocabulary to talk about experiences Express likes and dislikes Interview classmates Role-play Report research findings	Unstressed *to*	Word definitions Context clues Appropriate word usage	Verbs plus gerunds and infinitives
Make predictions Survey classmates Express opinions Act out scripted conversations Use new vocabulary in open conversation Use intonation to denote attitude Agree and disagree Ask and answer questions about daily habits Report on observation of gender roles	Rising and falling intonation patterns	Context clues Word definitions Idiomatic expressions	Adverbs and expressions of frequency
Make predictions Survey classmates Express opinions Compare and discuss solutions Politely express wants Role-play Discuss a shopping list Plan a dinner and report to class Present a restaurant review	Vowels [ʊ] and [uw]	Word definitions Synonyms Vocabulary classification Context clues Word association	Count and non-count nouns

Unit	Critical Thinking Skills	Listening Tasks

8
 An Ice Place to Stay
 Theme: Travel
 Listening One: *An Unusual Vacation*
    A travel hotline
 Listening Two: *Vacations Around the World*
    Three vacation packages
	Infer situational context
	 Interpret a map
	 Rank personal preferences in travel
	 Categorize information
	 Compare and contrast sounds
	 Evaluate vacation places according to different criteria
		Listen and predict
		 Listen for main ideas
		 Listen and categorize details
		 Interpret speaker's tone and attitude
		 Relate listenings to personal interests
		 Listen and take notes on student information
		 Connect themes between two listenings
		 Take dictation
		 Talk to travel agents to research a vacation place

9
 Staying Healthy
 Theme: Health and Illness
 Listening One: *Thin-Fast*
    A radio commercial
 Listening Two: *Health Problems and Remedies*
    Two conversations
	Interpret a cartoon
	 Assess personal health practices
	 Infer word meaning from context
	 Distinguish between opinion and fact
	 Rank student findings
		Listen and predict
		 Listen and identify main ideas
		 Listen for supporting details
		 Characterize speaker's tone
		 Listen to and take notes on conversations
		 Compare and contrast information from both listenings
		 Listen to and take notes on student commercials
		 Listen to and comment on student reports

10
 Endangered Languages
 Theme: Endangered Languages
 Listening One: *Language Loss*
    A class session
 Listening Two: *My Life, My Language*
    An autobiographical account
	Infer information not explicit in the text
	 Support opinion with reasoning
	 Hypothesize reasons
	 Correlate specific examples to broad themes
	 Summarize main ideas
	 Summarize and evaluate student findings
		Listen and predict
		 Listen and identify main ideas
		 Listen for details
		 Interpret speaker's tone
		 Link information from two texts using a graphic organizer
		 Relate listening to personal values
		 Listen to and take notes on student explanations

Speaking Tasks	Pronunciation	Vocabulary	Grammar
Make predictions Express opinions Make polite requests Role-play a conversation at an information desk Conduct an interview Agree and disagree Ask and answer travel questions Use new vocabulary in an open conversation Report research findings	*Can* and *can't*	Context clues Dictionary work Vocabulary classification	*Can* and *can't*
Brainstorm healthy practices Make predictions Express opinions Use new vocabulary in an open conversation Express concern about health problems Give and receive advice Role-play a radio commercial Interview people on health practices Report research findings	Rhythm: content words and highlighting	Word definitions Context clues	*Should, ought to,* and *have to*
Share background information Make predictions Express opinions Give examples to explain a general statement Survey classmates Interpret statistics Report findings on an endangered language	Using contractions with *will*	Word definitions Context clues Editing inaccurate definitions	Future with *will*

Acknowledgments

We would like to express our appreciation to the many people who helped make this project possible. Thanks go to Frances Boyd and Carol Numrich who helped us to narrow and shape our many ideas into the final text. Many thanks also go to Debbie Sistino and Françoise Leffler. Their guidance, input and editorial eyes were invaluable to us.

Finally, we would like to express our gratitude to Raymond Tucci, Stefan Frazier, and Merrilyn and Dewey Cedarblade for their patience and support as we put long hours into this work.

Robin Mills and *Laurie Frazier*

For her contribution in developing the NorthStar pronunciation syllabus, the publisher gratefully acknowledges the contribution of **Linda Lane**.

For the comments and insights they graciously offered to help shape the direction of the Second Edition of *NorthStar*, the publisher would like to thank all our **reviewers**. For a complete list of reviewers and institutions, see page 189.

Offbeat Jobs

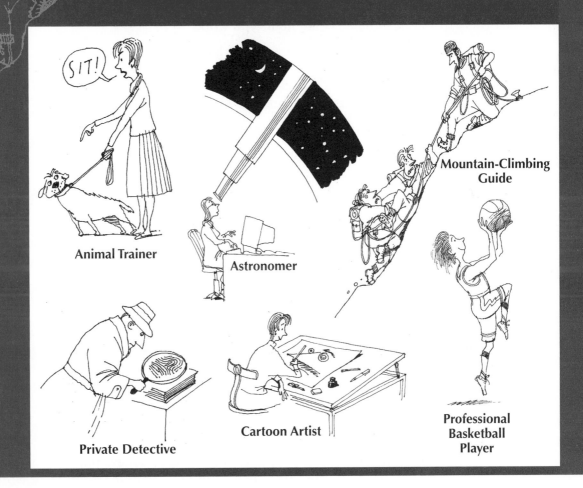

Animal Trainer

Astronomer

Mountain-Climbing Guide

Professional Basketball Player

Private Detective

Cartoon Artist

1 Focus on the Topic

A PREDICTING

Look at the pictures, and discuss these questions with the class.

1. What is each person doing?

2. Are these jobs ordinary, usual jobs or are they unusual?

3. Read the title of the unit. What does "offbeat" mean?

B　SHARING INFORMATION

1 *Look at the list of things to consider when choosing a job. Number the items in order of importance from **1** to **7**. Number 1 is the most important and number 7 is the least important.*

_____ **salary** (how much money you make)

_____ **hours** (what hours you work)

_____ **safety** (how safe the work is)

_____ **workplace** (indoors, outdoors, home, office)

_____ **interest** (how much you like the work)

_____ **education** (how much schooling you need for the job)

_____ **number of job openings** (how easy it is to find a job)

2 *Now work in a small group. Compare your answers. Tell why each item is important or not important to you.*

Examples:　Salary is important to me because I need to make money for my family.

Workplace isn't important to me because I can work anywhere—indoors, outdoors, at home, or in an office.

C　PREPARING TO LISTEN

BACKGROUND

When choosing a job, people need to consider many things. People should think about the salary. How much money does the job pay? They should also think about what the job is really like. For example, is it exciting, fun, or dangerous? It's a good idea for people to find a job that's right for them, to do work they enjoy and are good at doing.

1 *What's the job? Match the job in the box with the description in the chart on page 3. If you don't understand some of the words, use the dictionary or ask your teacher for help.*

animal trainer	cartoon artist	private detective
astronomer	mountain-climbing guide	professional basketball player

_____ job	_____ job	_____ job
$10,000	$25,000	$30,000
This job is exciting but dangerous. The people with this job like to work outdoors. They are athletic and adventurous, and they like to help other people.	This job is fun. The people with this job like to work with animals. They are patient and friendly. They also have to be careful because this job can be dangerous.	This job is often difficult and tiring. People with this job like to solve problems and help other people. They are hardworking and good at talking.
_____ job	_____ job	_____ job
$40,000	$80,000	$1,500,000
This is a fun job. The people with this job like to draw funny pictures. They are artistic and creative. They also like to work alone.	This job is interesting. The people with this job like to watch the stars. They are well educated. They are also good with numbers, computers, and telescopes.	This is a high-paying job, and it's fun. The people with this job like to play ball. They also like to work with other people. They are athletic and competitive.

2 *Now answer the following questions. Then compare your answers with a partner.*

1. Is there a job that you would like? Why?

Yes, I would like to be a/an _____ because it's

_____ .

2. Is this job right for you?

Yes. I am _____ .

I like _____ .

I also _____ .

(add your own ideas)

3. Is this a high-paying job? What's the salary?

_____

4. Should any of the jobs have a higher or lower salary? Why do you think so?

_____

VOCABULARY FOR COMPREHENSION

Read the sentences and guess the meanings of the underlined words.

1. I work in a computer <u>factory</u>. I help make computers.

2. I like to <u>taste</u> food while I'm cooking to make sure it is good.

3. Chefs are <u>creative</u>. They think of new ways to cook food.

4. I'm a dog walker. People are often surprised when I tell them my job because it's so <u>offbeat</u>.

5. I love ice cream because it has a sweet <u>flavor</u>.

6. I love to eat <u>spicy food</u> such as Thai food and Mexican food.

7. My friend was a <u>contestant</u> on a game show once. She answered some of the questions right and won $2,000.

8. I like to listen to a radio talk show every morning. The <u>host</u> is interesting, and she's funny.

9. I have sensitive <u>taste buds</u>. I don't like to eat spicy foods because they burn my mouth.

10. I have an <u>insurance policy</u> for my car. If I have an accident and my car is damaged, the insurance company will pay me some money.

Now match the words with their definitions.

_e_	**1.** factory	**a.** thinking of new ways of doing things
____	**2.** taste	**b.** an agreement with an insurance company to be paid money in case of an accident, illness, or death
____	**3.** creative	
____	**4.** offbeat	**c.** different or unusual
____	**5.** flavor	**d.** someone who plays a game
____	**6.** spicy food	**e.** a building where things are made
____	**7.** contestant	**f.** someone who talks to guests on a radio or TV program
____	**8.** host	
____	**9.** taste buds	**g.** particular taste of a food or drink
____	**10.** insurance policy	**h.** food with a strong flavor from spices
		i. try food by eating a little bit
		j. the parts of the tongue that can taste food

2 Focus on Listening

A ▎ LISTENING ONE: *What's My Job?*

🎧 *Listen to the beginning of "What's My Job?" Circle the correct answer to complete each statement.*

1. You are listening to a _____.
   a. job interview   **b.** game show   **c.** radio show

2. Wayne is a _____.
   a. host   **b.** contestant   **c.** guest

3. Rita is a _____.
   a. host   **b.** contestant   **c.** guest

4. Peter is going to describe _____.
   a. his job   **b.** his company   **c.** himself

5. Can you predict what Peter will talk about? (*Circle more than one answer.*)
   a. what he does   **b.** where he works   **c.** how much money he makes
   d. what he is like **e.** what he likes to do

LISTENING FOR MAIN IDEAS

🎧 *Now listen to the whole show. Circle the correct answer to complete each statement.*

1. Rita asks Peter _____ questions.
   a. two   **b.** three   **c.** four

2. Peter works in a _____.
   a. restaurant   **b.** factory   **c.** bakery

3. Peter is _____.
   a. a factory worker **b.** a chef   **c.** an ice-cream taster

4. Peter has to be careful with _____.
   a. his taste buds   **b.** the ice cream   **c.** the factory machines

5. Peter thinks his job is _____.
   a. tiring   **b.** great   **c.** dangerous

LISTENING FOR DETAILS

*Listen to "What's My Job?" again. Then read each statement and decide if it is true or false. Write **T** (true) or **F** (false) next to it.*

_____ 1. Peter can be creative at work.

_____ 2. Peter thinks of new ice-cream flavors.

_____ 3. He eats all the ice cream at work.

_____ 4. He doesn't eat spicy foods.

_____ 5. He doesn't drink alcohol or coffee.

_____ 6. He smokes.

_____ 7. He has a one-million-dollar insurance policy for his taste buds.

_____ 8. He studied ice-cream tasting in school.

Now go back to Section 2A (question 5) on page 5. Were your predictions correct?

REACTING TO THE LISTENING

1 *Listen to three excerpts from "What's My Job?" After listening to each excerpt, circle the correct word to complete each statement. Then answer the following question. Discuss your answers with the class.*

Excerpt One

1. Rita is _____.
   a. excited   **b.** calm
   How do you know?

2. Wayne wants Rita to _____ talking.
   a. continue   **b.** stop
   How do you know?

Excerpt Two

1. Wayne really thinks that Peter's job is _____.
   a. easy   **b.** difficult
   How do you know?

2. Peter thinks that Wayne is _____.
   a. serious   **b.** funny
   How do you know?

Excerpt Three

1. Wayne is trying to be _____.
   a. serious   **b.** funny
   How do you know?

2. Wayne really _____ that Peter went to ice-cream tasting school.
   a. thinks   **b.** doesn't think
   How do you know?

3. Peter is being _____.
   a. serious   **b.** funny
   How do you know?

2 *Discuss these questions with the class. Give your opinions.*

1. Do you think Peter's job is difficult or easy? Why do you think so?

2. Do you think you could do Peter's job?

3. Do you think it was easy for Peter to get started in his job? Why or why not?

B   LISTENING TWO: *More Offbeat Jobs*

1 *Look at the pictures above. Where does each person work? What job is each person doing?*

2 *Listen to the people talking about their jobs. Write the number of the conversation under the correct picture.*

3 *Listen again. Look at the statements in the chart. Write* **1** *if the statement is true for the window washer and* **2** *if the statement is true for the professional shopper. Some statements may be true for both.*

a. I like my job.	1, 2
b. I work outdoors.	
c. I earn a high salary.	
d. My work is dangerous.	
e. I like to work with people.	
f. I'm good with money.	
g. I'm good with my hands.	
h. My work is tiring.	
i. It was difficult to get started in this job.	
j. I have my own business.	

C   LINKING LISTENINGS ONE AND TWO

1 *You have learned about some unusual jobs. Read the questions below and write* **1, 2,** *or* **3** *for each one.*

1 = window washer   2 = professional shopper   3 = ice-cream taster

Which job do you think is . . .

_____ the most creative?   _____ the most difficult?

_____ the most tiring?   _____ the most important?

_____ the most relaxing?   _____ the most dangerous?

_____ the most offbeat?   _____ the highest paid?

2 *Now work in a small group. Explain your answers.*

Example: I think the ice-cream taster's job is the most offbeat because I don't think there are very many ice-cream tasters.

3 *Which job would you most like to have? Which job wouldn't you like to have? Explain.*

3 Focus on Vocabulary

1 *Complete the conversation with words from the box. Then work in pairs. Practice reading the conversation out loud with your partner. Change roles.*

be careful	high-paying	quit
get started	lucky	tiring
helping other people	offbeat	to work outdoors

A: So what do you do?

B: I'm a dog walker.

A: A dog walker? That's an unusual job!

B: Yes, it's an **(1)** _____ job.

A: So, how do you like it?

B: Oh, it's perfect for me because I love dogs, and I enjoy **(2)** _____.

A: So how did you **(3)** _____ as a dog walker?

B: Well, I used to walk my dog in the park every day. I met some people there with dogs. They asked me if I could walk their dogs for them.

A: That's great. So, do you have another job?

B: No, I used to be a computer programmer, but I got tired of working in an office. I decided I wanted **(4)** _____. So I **(5)** _____ my job to become a full-time dog walker. Now I only walk dogs. The only problem is that I don't make as much money. It's not a **(6)** _____ job.

A: Oh, I see. Is there anything else you don't like about it?

B: Well, it isn't easy. I have to walk a lot, so it's **(7)** _____ work. Also, some dogs can run fast. I have to **(8)** _____ not to let them get away. But even so, I really love it!

A: Good for you! You're **(9)** _____ to have a job you enjoy.

2 Work in pairs. Student A, read the first line of each conversation. Student B, respond to Student A. Make sure you use a word from the box below.

adventurous	get started	lucky	the right job for you
be careful	high-paying	offbeat	tiring
creative	indoors	outdoors	usual
dangerous	low-paying	safe	working alone

1. A: I want to find a new job. I don't want to work in an office anymore.

    B: *You want to work outdoors then.*

2. A: A friend of mine just got a job as a game-show host. I've never known a game-show host before.

    B: _____

3. A: I'm so excited because I just got the job I wanted. Over 40 other people were trying to get that job!

    B: _____

4. A: I don't think I would like to work in a factory. You have to watch your work very closely so you don't make mistakes.

    B: _____

5. A: I would like to work as a private detective, but I'm not sure how to find that kind of work.

    B: _____

Now change roles.

6. A: I think I'd like to become a nurse because I like helping others.

    B: _____

7. A: I can't believe how much money basketball players make. I wish I had such a big salary!

    B: _____

8. A: I love making up stories. Someday I want to write my own book.

    B: _____

9. A: Being a mountain-climbing guide sounds exciting, but I think I would be afraid of getting hurt. What do you think?

B: _____

10. A: I decided to become a teacher because I like school, and I enjoy helping other people.

B: _____

4 Focus on Speaking

A PRONUNCIATION: Stress

In words with more than one syllable, one syllable is stressed. Stressed syllables sound longer than unstressed syllables. They are also louder and higher in pitch than unstressed syllables.

 Listen to these examples:

<u>care</u>ful
cre<u>a</u>tive
ad<u>ven</u>turous

A compound noun is formed when two nouns are used together as one noun. In compound nouns, the stress is usually stronger on the first word in the compound.

 Listen to these examples:

<u>ani</u>mal trainer
<u>sales</u>clerk

When an adjective is followed by a noun, the stress is usually stronger on the noun.

 Listen to these examples:

professional <u>shop</u>per
good <u>pay</u>

1 *Listen to the words. Write the number of syllables you hear in each word. Then listen again and underline the stressed syllable. Listen again and repeat the words.*

_____ 1. dangerous

_____ 2. important

_____ 3. relaxing

_____ 4. educated

_____ 5. artistic

_____ 6. patient

_____ 7. unusual

_____ 8. interesting

2 *Read each item and underline the stressed syllable. Listen and check your answers. Then work with a partner. Take turns saying each item and listening for the correct stress.*

1. private detective

2. window washer

3. high salary

4. taste buds

5. ice cream

6. spicy foods

7. department store

3 *Work in pairs. Student A, ask questions with the phrases on the left. Student B, answer with the phrases on the right. Be sure to use the correct stress. Change roles after item 4.*

Example: A: What do you call someone who washes windows?

B: A window washer.

1. someone who washes windows   **a.** taste bud

2. a frozen dessert   **b.** window washer

3. someone who sells things   **c.** dog walker

4. someone who draws cartoons   **d.** cartoon artist

5. a list of things you need to buy   **e.** ice cream

6. someone who solves crimes   **f.** shopping list

7. a part of the tongue you taste food with   **g.** private detective

8. someone who walks dogs   **h.** salesclerk

B   STYLE: Small Talk

When making conversation, it's polite to ask about a person's job and interests (what people like to do in their free time). It's also polite to express interest (to react positively) when people tell you something about themselves.

Asking about someone's job and interests	Talking about yourself	Showing interest
What do you do?	I'm not working right now. I'm a (student/chef/homemaker). I'm retired.*	Oh … Really?
How do you like it?	It's great. It's interesting. It's all right, but … I don't like it at all.	Good for you. Oh, I see. Oh, no. Why not?
What do you like to do in your free time?	I like to (listen to music/play tennis). I enjoy (reading/playing computer games).	That's interesting. That's nice.

Work in pairs. Complete the conversation with your own information. Then practice it out loud.

A: Hi. My name's _____.

B: Hi. I'm _____. Nice to meet you.

A: Nice to meet you, too. So what do you do?

B: I'm _____.

A: _____. How do you like it?

B: _____. How about you? What do you do?

A: _____.

B: _____. So what do you like to do in your free time?

A: _____. How about you?

B: _____.

---

* ***retired:*** no longer working at a job, usually because of age

C GRAMMAR: Descriptive Adjectives

1 Work in pairs. Read the conversations out loud. Notice the underlined words. Then answer the questions below.

1. A: What's your job like?

   B: My job is <u>interesting</u>.

2. A: What kind of person are you?

   B: I'm a <u>friendly</u> person.

a. Look at the answers to the questions. What is the verb in each sentence?

b. What is the noun in each sentence?

c. Which words describe the nouns? Where do they come in the sentences?

Descriptive Adjectives

Adjectives describe nouns.

1. Adjectives can come after the verb **be**.

   My job **is *tiring*.**

2. Adjectives can also come before a noun.

   Artists are ***creative* people.**

3. When a singular noun follows an adjective, use **a** before the adjective if the adjective begins with a consonant sound.

   This isn't **a *high-paying* job.**

4. When a singular noun follows an adjective, use **an** before the adjective if the adjective begins with a vowel sound.

   Peter has **an *unusual* job.**

2 Work in pairs. Take turns making statements using the nouns and adjectives provided. After one of you makes a statement, the other one reacts, saying, "I agree" or "I don't agree." If you don't agree with a statement, correct it.

Example: a secretary's work / dangerous

   A: A secretary's work is dangerous.

   B: I don't agree. A secretary's work isn't dangerous. It's safe.

1. a mountain-climbing guide's job / tiring

2. an ice-cream taster / creative person

3. a professional basketball player's work / difficult

4. private detectives / patient people

5. window washing / interesting job

6. animal training / important work

7. a professional shopper's job / relaxing

D SPEAKING TOPICS

Work in pairs. Your partner is looking for a job. Follow these steps.

1. Interview your partner. Ask him or her the following questions. If your partner's answer is **yes,** he or she should explain. Write the answers.

Example: A: Are you artistic?

B: Yes, I am. I can draw.

A: Do you like to work alone?

B: Yes, I do. I don't like to work with people.

Are you ...	Yes	No	Explain
artistic?			
athletic?			
careful?			
hardworking?			
friendly?			
good with numbers?			
good with your hands?			
good with languages?			

Do you like to ...	Yes	No	Explain
work alone?			
work with animals?			
work outdoors?			
work in an office?			
help people?			
make things?			
solve problems?			

2. Choose a job that you think is good for your partner. Think of a job from the unit or a different one.

3. Introduce your partner to the class. Tell the class which job you think is good for your partner and use the information in the chart to tell why.

Listening Task

As you listen to your classmates, write down the names of two students who are like you or like doing the same things you do. Do you agree with the jobs their partners recommend?

Student's Name	Student Is	Student Likes	Job

E RESEARCH TOPIC

Would you like to find an offbeat job? Follow these steps.

1. Work in a small group. Think of some offbeat jobs and make a list. You can include jobs from the unit or other offbeat jobs that you know.

2. Now, work alone. Choose one offbeat job or a job you would like to have. Go to the library, look on the Internet, or interview someone who does the job to get information about it. Take notes. Your notes should include the information below.

Job title: _____

Workplace: _____

Person has to be: _____

Person has to like: _____

Why the job is interesting: _____

3. Report to the class.

Listening Task

Listen to your classmates' reports. Which job do you think is the most interesting?

For Unit 1 Internet activities, visit the NorthStar Companion Website at http://www.longman.com/northstar.

A Piece of the Country in the City

1 Focus on the Topic

A PREDICTING

Look at the picture, and discuss these questions with the class.

1. Which parts of the picture are the city, the suburbs, and the country? Point to them. How do you know?

2. Read the title of the unit. What do you think it means?

17

B SHARING INFORMATION

Work in a small group. Discuss these questions. Use the words in the box to help you.

apartments	gardens	nature	stores
crowded	highways	neighborhoods	tall buildings
dangerous	houses	quiet	traffic
farms	malls	safe	trees

1. How is the city different from the suburbs? How is it different from the country?

The city is _____.   The city has _____.

The country is _____.   The country has _____.

The suburbs are _____.   The suburbs have _____.

2. Which place do you prefer? Why?

C PREPARING TO LISTEN

BACKGROUND

1 *Look at the graph. Then answer the questions below.*

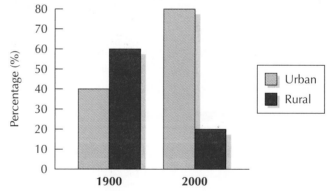

City/Country Population in the United States in 1900 and 2000

Source: U.S. Census Bureau

1. What percent of the population lived in the country in 1900?

2. What percent of the population lived in the city in 1900?

3. What percent of the population lived in the country in 2000?

4. What percent of the population lived in the city in 2000?

5. What change do you see? Why has the change happened?

2 *Read the paragraphs. Then work in a small group. Read each statement in the chart below. Check (✓) if it is true or false. If it is false, correct it. Use the paragraphs to help you.*

In 1900, 60 percent of the people in the United States lived in the country and 40 percent lived in the city. By 2000, 80 percent of the population was urban, or lived in the city, and only 20 percent was rural, or lived in the country. With more and more people living in cities, cities are getting bigger. Bigger cities often mean fewer green areas. Now, more cities are starting programs called "urban greening." Urban greening programs create more green areas in cities. Urban greening programs make places for people to enjoy nature. Urban greening is a way to have a little piece of the country in the city.

Parks and gardens are examples of urban greening programs. In 1895, about 20 cities in the United States started vegetable gardens to grow food to help feed poor people. Later, more and more city people started having vegetable gardens. Soon, many people in neighborhoods had *community gardens,* gardens where people work together to grow vegetables and flowers. In 1996, there were over 6,000 community gardens in 38 cities throughout the United States.

Statement	True	False	Correction
1. Urban greening programs bring the city to the country.			
2. The first city gardens grew vegetables and flowers.			
3. Community gardens are gardens neighborhood people share.			
4. Community gardens grow food to help feed the poor.			

VOCABULARY FOR COMPREHENSION

Read the sentences and guess the meanings of the underlined words.

1. I saw a beautiful <u>community garden</u> today. Many people worked together and made one large garden.

2. People can <u>grow</u> many things in a garden. Some people grow vegetables. Other people grow flowers.

3. There are many apartment buildings and houses on my street, but one area doesn't have any buildings on it. It's an <u>empty lot</u>. There's nothing there.

4. Many people in my neighborhood enjoy their gardens. They put many things in their gardens. They <u>plant</u> vegetables and flowers.

5. Sometimes people throw paper, empty soda cans, and other <u>garbage</u> on the ground. It's better to put it in a garbage can.

6. I live in a small house, but there is a nice big <u>yard</u> behind my house. I enjoy sitting outside in my yard.

7. There is an old tree in front of my house. I will take the tree away. I will <u>remove</u> it.

8. Some people use <u>drugs</u>. Some drugs, like medicines, are good. Other drugs are dangerous and illegal.

9. I enjoy trees, flowers, and the mountains. I really like <u>nature</u>.

10. On the weekends, my family likes to go to <u>the country</u>. We drive for a few hours far away from the city so we can enjoy the trees and plants.

Now match the words with their definitions.

<u> i </u> **1.** community garden

____ **2.** grow

____ **3.** empty lot

____ **4.** plant

____ **5.** garbage

____ **6.** yard

____ **7.** remove

____ **8.** drugs

____ **9.** nature

____ **10.** the country

a. take away

b. to have flowers or vegetables in a garden

c. trees, flowers, mountains, and other things outside

d. paper and other things people don't want anymore

e. an area of land next to or behind a house

f. a place far from the city where people go to enjoy nature

g. something like medicines but dangerous and illegal, like cocaine

h. to put seeds in the ground to become flowers or vegetables

i. a garden that many people make together

j. an area of land with no buildings on it

A community garden in New York City

2 Focus on Listening

A LISTENING ONE: *Community Gardens*

 Listen to Laura Lee talking about community gardens. Read each question. Then circle the correct answer.

1. What are you listening to?
   a. a TV news show
   b. a radio news show
   c. a phone conversation

2. Where is Laura Lee?
   a. in the radio studio
   b. in her yard
   c. at a community garden

3. What do you think she will learn about community gardens? (*Circle more than one answer.*)
   a. what the people plant
   b. what people do in community gardens
   c. how many community gardens are in New York
   d. why the garden is important

LISTENING FOR MAIN IDEAS

 Read this list of reasons to have a community garden. Listen to the complete radio interview. Check (✓) the reasons the man gives to reporter Laura Lee.

_____ 1. Community gardens make neighborhoods look nice.

_____ 2. Community gardens are good places for people to enjoy nature.

_____ 3. Community gardens are good places to walk dogs.

_____ 4. Community gardens are good places to grow food.

_____ 5. Community gardens are good places to grow flowers to sell.

LISTENING FOR DETAILS

*Listen to the complete radio interview again. Then read each statement and decide if it is true or false. Write **T** (true) or **F** (false) next to it.*

_____ 1. Ten years ago this was an empty lot.

_____ 2. One person in the neighborhood planted the community garden.

_____ 3. Before the garden, there was garbage on the empty lot.

_____ **4.** There are enough apartment buildings in New York.

_____ **5.** The neighbors made the neighborhood a nice place to live.

_____ **6.** Before the garden, there wasn't a place to sit and relax.

_____ **7.** Now, people sell vegetables, not drugs.

_____ **8.** The man grew up in the country.

_____ **9.** The man has a yard at his apartment building.

_____ **10.** Tomorrow night the radio show will be about the city's plans.

Now go back to Section 2A (question 3) on page 21. Were your predictions correct?

REACTING TO THE LISTENING

 1 *Listen to two excerpts from the radio interview. After listening to each excerpt, read each question and circle the correct answer.*

Excerpt One

1. How did the man feel about the place before they planted the garden?
   a. He enjoyed it.   **b.** He thought it was nice.   **c.** He didn't like it.

2. How does the man feel about the city's plans?
   a. He is happy.   **b.** He is unhappy.   **c.** He is excited.

3. What words does he use to tell you his feelings?
   a. "I can't believe it."   **b.** "We made it beautiful."

Excerpt Two

1. Did the neighborhood have a park before the community garden? Which phrase tells you?
   a. This neighborhood didn't have trees or flowers.
   b. Children didn't have a place to play either.

2. What does this phrase mean: "We have a small part of the country in the city"?
   a. The garden is small.
   b. The garden is similar to the country.

2 *Discuss these questions with the class. Give your opinions.*

1. What do you think the city of New York will do about the community garden in Listening One? Why?

2. What kind of urban greening programs does your city have? How do people use them?

3. What urban greening programs do you think a city should have? Why?

B LISTENING TWO: *Let's Hear from Our Listeners*

1 *Work with a partner. Before you listen to "Let's Hear from Our Listeners," look at the pictures. Then read the questions in the chart and write short answers in the "Before you listen" column.*

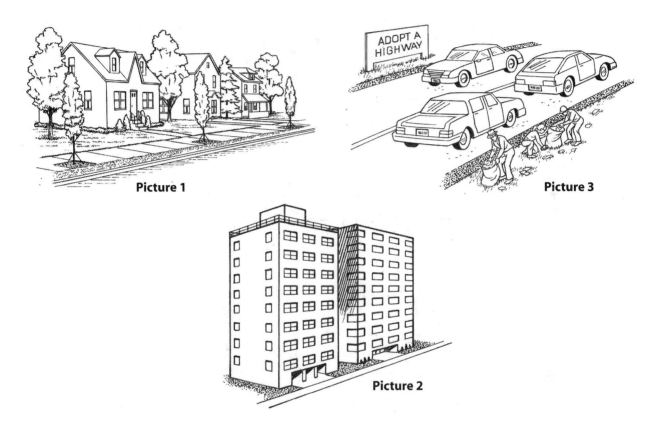

Picture 1

Picture 3

Picture 2

	Before you listen	**After you listen**
1. Who do you think planted the trees in Picture 1?		
2. Do you think there is a garden in Picture 2? Where?		
3. What are the people doing in Picture 3? Why?		

2 *Now listen to the radio call-in show. Then read the questions in the chart again. Write your answers in the "After you listen" column. Compare your "before" and "after" answers. Were your "before" answers correct?*

C   LINKING LISTENINGS ONE AND TWO

Work in a group of three students. Look at the chart below. It lists the urban greening programs talked about in this unit. Discuss each kind of urban greening program and how it can be done.

	Community gardens	Roof gardens	Trees on streets	City parks
Individuals can do this because …				
Groups of neighbors can do this because …				
Cities can do this because …				
This is expensive to do because …				
This is easy to do because …				
This is a good urban greening program for my city because …				

3 Focus on Vocabulary

1 *Match the words on the left with the definitions on the right.*

   d   1. community garden

_____ 2. empty lot

_____ 3. get together

_____ 4. grow up

_____ 5. hang around

_____ 6. roof garden

_____ 7. urban greening

_____ 8. relax

a. putting green areas in a city; parks and gardens

b. not work, have free time to rest

c. a garden on top of a building

d. a garden many people grow together

e. stay in one place not doing anything

f. an area with no buildings on it

g. become an adult; get older

h. meet with people

2 *Complete the conversation with words from Exercise 1. Use the underlined words to help you. Then work in pairs. Practice reading the conversation out loud with your partner. Change roles.*

A: Good afternoon. This is *Radio Call In* on WNYZ. How can I help you today?

B: Well, my neighborhood really needs something to <u>make it more beautiful and green</u>.

A: Hmm. So you are looking for ideas about (**1**) _____?

B: Yes. Do you have any ideas?

A: Well, there are many things you can do. First of all, you should try to <u>meet with all your neighbors</u>.

B: OK. I'll try to (**2**) _____ with everyone.

A: Then you can discuss ideas. For example, you can plant <u>gardens on top of the apartment buildings</u>.

B: OK, maybe a (**3**) _____. That's a good idea.

A: Yes, and people can go there after work to just <u>sit and rest</u>.

B: Yes, that would be a nice place to (**4**) _____.

A: Or if there is <u>an area with no buildings on it</u>, you could plant a community garden.

B: Yes, we have an (**5**) _____. And now, a lot of people <u>stand there doing nothing</u>.

A: Yes, people will (**6**) _____ empty lots.

B: These are good ideas. Thanks. You know, when I was a child, I lived in the country and we had a lot of green areas. Then, when I <u>became an adult</u>, I moved to the city. Things sure are different here!

A: Yes, things change when we (**7**) _____. Well, I hope you use some urban greening ideas in your neighborhood.

B: OK, I will. Thanks. Bye-bye.

3 *Work in pairs. Do a role play discussing an urban greening program described below. Student A is a city official and Student B is a neighbor. Use the questions and the vocabulary listed. Then do it again, changing roles.*

Urban Greening Program

Your city owns an empty lot. A group of neighbors wants to make it a community garden. One neighbor talks to a city official about the idea.

Example: A: What is your <u>urban greening</u> program?

B: We have an <u>empty lot</u> near our building, so we want to make a <u>community garden</u>.

A: Why do you want to make a <u>community garden</u>?

B: We need a nice place to <u>get together</u> with friends and neighbors.

A: . . .

Questions

What is your _____ program?

Why do you want to _____ ?

How will you _____ ?

What can _____ do to help?

Vocabulary

community garden
drugs
empty lot
get together
grow
hang around
nature
plant
relax
urban greening

4 Focus on Speaking

A PRONUNCIATION: Pronunciation of Past Tense

The regular past tense is written by adding *-ed* to a verb. For example, *walk* becomes *walked*. The regular past tense has three pronunciations: /t/, /d/, and /əd/ or /ɪd/. The pronunciation depends on the last sound in the base verb.

 Listen to these examples:

I want**ed** to work in the garden yesterday.
I look**ed** at the garden this morning.
The children play**ed** in the park.

PRONUNCIATION OF PAST TENSE		
1 wanted	**2 looked**	**3 played**
Pronounce -ed as /əd/ or /ɪd/ when the verb ends in /t/ and /d/. The -ed ending is a new syllable.	Pronounce -ed as /t/ when the verb ends in these sounds: /p/, /k/, /f/, /s/, /ʃ/, /tʃ/.	Pronounce -ed as /d/ when the verb ends in any other consonant or in a vowel.
🎧 Listen:	🎧 Listen:	🎧 Listen:
wanted	looked	played
visited	missed	lived
ended	watched	listened

1 *Pronounce these verbs. Look at the chart above to help you choose the correct pronunciation. Circle the number of the correct pronunciation next to the verbs. When you are finished, check your answers with a partner.*

Base Form	Regular Past Tense	Correct Pronunciation		
a. stay	stayed	1	2	3
b. laugh	laughed	1	2	3
c. wait	waited	1	2	3
d. talk	talked	1	2	3
e. decide	decided	1	2	3
f. love	loved	1	2	3

 2 *Underline the verb in each sentence. Then listen to these sentences and write the verb under the correct sound in the chart on page 28. Finally, read the sentences aloud.*

1. I <u>worked</u> in the community garden yesterday.

2. She planted some vegetables last week.

3. My children played on an empty lot near my home.

4. I walked on a beautiful tree-lined street today.

5. Last week, the city removed garbage from an empty lot.

6. Everyone liked the flowers in the community garden.

7. My family lived in the city last year.

8. They stayed in the garden until evening yesterday.

9. I wanted to visit the country last weekend.

10. We watched some children playing.

/ɪd/	/t/	/d/
	worked	

3 *Think of two more verbs for the different pronunciations of the past tense ending. Write them under the correct sound. Compare your answers with a partner.*

B ▐ STYLE: **Expressing Agreement**

Expressing Agreement

1. In conversation, when we want to agree with an affirmative statement someone has just made, we can use the word **too** in our response.

    A: I like gardens.
    B: I like gardens, **too.**

2. When we want to agree with a negative statement someone has just made, we can use **not ... either** in our response.

    A: I don't live in the country.
    B: I do**n't** live in the country, **either.**

Work in pairs. Read these conversations. Circle the correct word to complete each response. Then practice reading the conversations out loud. Change roles with each conversation.

1. A: I work in a city.

    B: I work in a city, <u>either / too</u>.

2. A: My family doesn't live in this city.

    B: My family doesn't live here, <u>either / too</u>.

3. A: I lived in the suburbs when I was a child.

   B: I lived in the suburbs, <u>either / too</u>.

4. A: I didn't have a garden three years ago.

   B: I didn't have a garden, <u>too / either</u>.

5. A: My apartment doesn't have a yard.

   B: My apartment doesn't have a yard, <u>either / too</u>.

6. A: I like to grow flowers.

   B: I like to grow flowers, <u>too / either</u>.

7. A: My neighborhood doesn't have a community garden.

   B: My neighborhood doesn't have one, <u>too / either</u>.

8. A: There's a yard behind my house.

   B: There's a yard behind my house, <u>too / either</u>.

C   GRAMMAR: Simple Past Tense

1 *Work in pairs. Read the conversations out loud. Then answer the questions below.*

1. A: I relaxed in the garden yesterday.

   B: Well . . . I worked. I planted vegetables.

2. A: She didn't plant flowers last week.

   B: He didn't plant flowers, either.

3. A: Last year, they grew vegetables.

   B: Last year, we grew vegetables, too.

a. Do the sentences talk about the past, the present, or the future? How do you know?

b. Underline the verbs. Which verbs are regular? Which are irregular? How do you know?

Simple Past Tense

1. Use the simple past tense to talk about an event that happened in the past.

We **planted** this garden ten years ago. Last year, we **bought** it from the city.

2. To form the simple past tense of regular verbs, add **-d** or **-ed** to the base form.

Sometimes there are spelling changes.

Base Form	Simple Past
live	live**d**
work	work**ed**
try	tr**ied**
plan	pla**nned**

3. Many verbs have irregular past tense forms. Here are some:

Base Form	Simple Past
buy	**bought**
get	**got**
give	**gave**
grow	**grew**
have	**had**
make	**made**
sell	**sold**

4. The verb form is the same for all persons, except with the verb **be**.

I **planted** flowers last summer.
She **planted** flowers, too.
It **was** a beautiful garden.
The trees **were** very tall.

5. To form a negative statement, use **did not** or **didn't** + base form of the verb, except with the verb *be*.

I **didn't live** in the suburbs last year.
She **didn't have** a garden.
It **wasn't** a nice place.
We **weren't** happy.

6. **Time markers** for the past tense come at the beginning or the end of the sentence.

Yesterday, I walked in the country.
I went to the city **last week.**

Other time markers:

yesterday morning / afternoon / evening
the day / week / month / night **before**
last week / Sunday / summer / night
a week / month / year **ago**

2 *Complete this news report with the simple past tense form of the verbs. Then practice reading the report out loud with a partner. Change roles.*

DAN: Good evening, I'm Dan Walters, welcoming you to *Interesting Information about New York*. Tonight, we have an interesting story about gardens in New York. I'm sure you've heard of the famous actress Bette Midler. But did you know how she saved the community gardens of New York? Here is our reporter Kate Rather with the story. Kate . . .

KATE: Well, Dan, in 1996, Bette Midler _____ an
                                                   1. (start)
organization called New York Restoration Project (NYRP). She

_____ to help improve urban greening in New York.
              2. (want)
NYRP _____ parks and _____
               3. (clean)   4. (pick up)
garbage in neighborhoods in New York.

In 1999, the city of New York _____ to sell
                                         5. (decide)
114 lots with community gardens. NYRP and other groups

_____ together and _____ to
            6. (get)   7. (plan)
save the gardens. They _____ more than $5 million
                                 8. (raise)
to buy the gardens.

On May 13, 1999, when the city of New York

_____ the 114 community gardens, NYRP and the
             9. (sell)
groups _____ 63 of the gardens. Then Bette Midler
                 10. (buy)
_____ 51 more gardens with her own money! The
           11. (buy)
114 gardens _____ saved!
                 12. (be)

3 *Read the timeline. It tells how Bette Midler helped save a great number of community gardens in New York.*

Famous Actress and Local Groups Save 114 Community Gardens

Bette Midler (center) *in a clean-up action in a New York City park.*

1994	Bette Midler and her family move to New York Bette Midler wants to help beautify the city
1996	Bette Midler starts organization called New York Restoration Project (NYRP) NYRP hires many workers to clean up New York NYRP cleans up many New York parks NYRP picks up garbage in neighborhoods
1999	City of New York decides to sell 114 community gardens NYRP and other groups get together to save community gardens NYRP donates $1 million Bette Midler gives $250,000 NYRP and other groups raise $5 million to buy community gardens
May 13, 1999	City of New York sells 114 community gardens NYRP and other groups buy 63 gardens Bette Midler buys 51 gardens with her own money Bette Midler, NYRP, and other groups save community gardens

Work in pairs. Take turns making statements about the timeline and reacting to the statements. Student A, make a statement. Student B, react by saying, "That's right," or "That's wrong." If the statement is wrong, say why and correct it. Use the past tense.

Examples: A: In 1996, NYRP cleaned up many New York parks.

B: That's right.

B: In 1999, Bette Midler gave $25,000.

A: That's wrong. She didn't give $25,000. She gave $250,000.

4 *First, look at the chart below. Write past tense statements about yourself for each activity. They can be affirmative or negative. Then add two more activities and write past tense statements.*

Activities	_____ name	_____ name	_____ name	_____ name
1. walk in the / park this morning	I walked in the park this morning.			
2. yesterday / get together with friends				
3. relax at home / last week				
4. last year / live in a city				
5.				
6.				

*Next, work in groups of four. One student reads a statement from his or her chart. The other students make a statement to express agreement using **too** or **not … either**. (If you don't agree, make a past tense statement about what you did.) Write the responses in the chart.*

Example: A: I walked in the park this morning.

B: I walked in the park this morning, too.

C: I didn't walk in the park this morning. I went to the gym.

D: I didn't walk in the park, either. I stayed home.

D   SPEAKING TOPICS

What is your favorite place? What is your partner's favorite place? Find out. Follow these steps.

1. Think of a place where you like to go to enjoy nature. It may be your yard, a park in your city, the country, or a place you have been for vacation. Answer the questions on a separate piece of paper. You can bring a picture of the place to show other students.

   PLACE: _____

   a. Is the place in the city, the suburbs, or the country?

   b. When did you go there? Why did you go?

   c. What did you see there? Describe it.

   d. What did you do there? Describe your activities.

   e. How did you find out about the place? (e.g., Did a friend tell you?)

   f. Is there other information you want to add?

2. Work in pairs. Have a conversation about your places. Student A begins by answering the first question. Student B answers the first question and makes a statement about his or her place. Use *too* or *not . . . either* if you agree with your partner.

   Examples: A: I went to a park—Golden Gate Park in San Francisco.

   B: I went to a park, too. I went to Tivoli Gardens in Copenhagen.

   OR

   A: I didn't go to a place in the city. I went to the country—to a farm in Wyoming.

   B: I didn't go to a place in the city, either. I went to a ranch in Texas.

3. Try to remember what your partner just told you about his or her place. If there are details that you can't remember, ask him or her, using the questions above, and take notes.

4. Tell the class about your partner's place.

Listening Task

Listen to your classmates' reports. Write down three places where you want to go. Why do you want to go there, too?

E RESEARCH TOPIC

You're going to research the urban greening programs in your city or town. Work in small groups. Follow these steps.

1. Each group goes to a different neighborhood and tries to answer these questions. Take notes.

   a. How many gardens did you see?

   b. How many community gardens did you see?

   c. How many roof gardens did you see?

   d. What do people grow?

   e. Did you see trees planted on the street?

   f. What other urban greening or city beautification programs did you see?

2. Report to the class about what you saw.

Listening Task

Listen to your classmates' reports and write down the information in the chart below. Which is the greenest neighborhood in your city?

Neighborhood	Gardens	Community gardens	Roof gardens	What do people grow?	Trees on the street	Other urban greening programs

For Unit 2 Internet activities, visit the NorthStar Companion Website at http://www.longman.com/northstar.

A Penny Saved
Is a Penny Earned

1 Focus on the Topic

A PREDICTING

Look at the picture, and discuss these questions with the class.

1. What is the man's problem?

2. What do you think he should do?

3. Read the title of the unit. It is a famous American saying. What do you think it means?

B   SHARING INFORMATION

1 *How do you usually pay for the things you need? Label each way to pay for things by writting **O** (often), **S** (sometimes), or **N** (never).*

_____ **cash**

_____ **checks**

_____ **credit cards** (plastic cards used to buy things and pay later)

_____ **loans** (borrowed money that you pay back later)

2 *Now work in a small group. Answer these questions.*

1. In your group, what is the most common way to pay for things? What is the least common?

2. What do you think is the best way to pay for things when you want to save money? Why do you think so?

C   PREPARING TO LISTEN

BACKGROUND

1 *Look at the timeline. Then discuss the questions below with the class.*

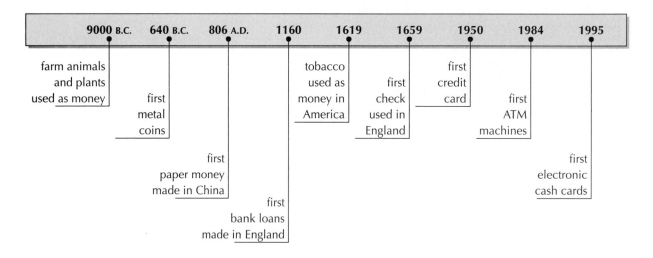

1. What is the oldest form of money? What is the newest?

2. What are the advantages and disadvantages of each kind?

3. Why do you think farm animals and tobacco were used as money?

4. Why did people start to use bank loans and credit cards to pay for things?

2 *Read the paragraph. Then discuss the questions below with a partner. Compare your answers with the class.*

Before people used money, they got the things they needed by bartering. Bartering is trading one thing for another without using money. For example, in the past, people might have traded some food for some clothing. Today, people, businesses, and governments still barter as a way to save money. Some people use the Internet to barter. Also, people in city neighborhoods and communities are starting to use barter networks. A barter network is a group of people in a town or city that trade with each other. A barter network helps people to save money and get to know others in their community.

1. What is bartering?

2. How long have people bartered?

VOCABULARY FOR COMPREHENSION

1 *Read each statement. Then circle the correct definition of the underlined word.*

1. Today I joined a health club. Now I'm a <u>member</u>, so I can go there to exercise or play sports.

a. a healthy person   **b.** a person who belongs to a group

2. I bought a new coat, but it's the wrong size. Today, I'm going back to the store to <u>exchange</u> it for another one.

a. trade something for something else   **b.** buy a new thing

3. The school <u>provides</u> breakfast for its students; they eat there every morning.

a. gives something to someone   **b.** gets something from someone

4. A check isn't the same as cash. It just <u>represents</u> the money that you pay.

a. is a sign for something   **b.** pays for something

5. She <u>earns</u> a big salary. She earns $250,000 a year.

a. pays money   **b.** gets money by working

6. I like to <u>spend</u> money. I like to buy lots of things.

a. pay money for things   **b.** get money by working

7. My co-workers and I receive <u>equal</u> salaries. We both earn $45,000 a year.

a. the same   **b.** large

8. His work has been <u>valuable</u> to our business. He has helped our business grow.

a. useful or important   **b.** expensive

9. Reading and writing are important <u>skills</u> for students to have.

a. things you do well   **b.** things that are difficult

2 Focus on Listening

A   LISTENING ONE: *A Barter Network*

 Listen to the beginning of "A Barter Network." Then read each question and circle the correct answer.

1. What are you listening to?
   a. a radio announcement
   b. a meeting
   c. a class

2. Who is listening to Carol speak?
   a. members of the barter network
   b. people who work for the barter network
   c. people who are interested in joining the network

3. Can you predict what topics Carol is going to discuss? (*Circle more than one answer.*)
   a. what bartering is
   b. why people like to barter
   c. how to use the barter network
   d. how to join the network

4. What information do you think Carol is going to provide? (*Circle everything you think you'll hear about.*)
   a. examples of things people barter
   b. how old the barter network is
   c. how many members belong to the network
   d. names of other members
   e. how to find other members
   f. an example of a barter exchange

LISTENING FOR MAIN IDEAS

 *Listen to the whole barter network meeting. Then read each statement and decide if it is true or false. Write **T** (true) or **F** (false) next to it.*

_____   1. In this group, members barter for services.

_____   2. Members only provide services that a lot of people need.

_____   3. You can earn money for providing services.

_____   4. You can use Time Dollars to buy services.

LISTENING FOR DETAILS

 One person took notes at the meeting. Listen to the whole meeting again. Fill in the missing information.

<u>CITY BARTER NETWORK</u>

A. <u>What do members barter?</u>
- Services—things they can _____ for other people.

B. <u>How does it work?</u>
- Sign a member list.
- List services you can _____.
- Get the list or read it on the Website.

C. <u>What kinds of services do members provide?</u>
- Services that a lot of people need—Ex., cooking, cleaning, _____ things.
- Some unusual services—Ex., taking photographs, tutoring, giving _____ lessons.

D. <u>How do you barter?</u>
1. Provide a service
   - One hour of work—you _____ one Time Dollar.
   - Time Dollars _____ hours worked.
2. Spend Time Dollars to get services
   - Everyone's time is _____.
<u>Example:</u>
   - Carol spent _____ hours cleaning—she earned three Time Dollars.
   - Someone fixed her TV—she spent _____ Time Dollar(s).
   - She _____ money.

E. <u>My Skills:</u>
- Dog-_____.

Now go back to Section 2A (questions 3 and 4) on page 40. Were your predictions correct?

REACTING TO THE LISTENING

 1 *Listen to three excerpts from the barter network meeting. After listening to each excerpt, read the first question and circle the correct answer. Then answer the following questions. Discuss your answers with the class.*

Excerpt One

1. How does the man feel about exchanging services?
   a. He feels excited.
   b. He doesn't feel excited.

2. How do you know?

3. Why do you think he feels that way?

Excerpt Two

1. How does the woman feel about getting piano lessons?
   a. She feels excited.
   b. She doesn't feel excited.

2. How do you know?

3. Why do you think she feels that way?

Excerpt Three

1. How does the man feel?
   a. He feels excited.
   b. He doesn't feel excited.

2. How do you know?

3. Why do you think he feels that way?

2 *Discuss these questions with the class. Give your opinions.*

1. Do you have a barter network in your community? Would you like to join a barter network? Why or why not?

2. Bartering is one way to save money. Do you prefer to save your money or spend your money? Why?

B   LISTENING TWO: *Saving Money*

 1 *Work with a partner. Look at the pictures and describe them to your partner. Then listen to the conversations. Circle the number of each conversation next to the correct picture in the chart.*

Picture A

Picture B

Picture C

Conversation	What did the person buy?	How much did the person save?
1 2 3		
1 2 3		
1 2 3		

 2 *Listen again. What did each person buy? How much money did each person save? Write your answers in the chart.*

C   LINKING LISTENINGS ONE AND TWO

You have heard about some different ways to save money:

- Bartering

- Buying used things at thrift stores

- Shopping at factory outlet stores

- Shopping on the Internet

Work in a small group. Discuss these questions.

1. Have you tried any of them? If not, would you like to?

2. What are the benefits of each way to save money? What are some problems?

3. What do you think is the best way to save money? Why do you think so?

3 Focus on Vocabulary

1 *Complete the conversations with words from the box. Use the underlined words to help you. Then work in pairs. Practice reading the conversations out loud with your partner. Change roles after item 4.*

a good deal	exchange	unusual
cheap	regular price	used
compare	stuff	valuable

1. A: I bought a chair at a thrift store yesterday. It <u>isn't new</u>, but it's very nice.

   B: Do you really like to buy _____ things?

2. A: Was the chair <u>inexpensive</u>?

   B: Yes, it was _____.

3. A: I always buy clothes on sale. I never pay the <u>full price</u>.

   B: Really? You never buy clothes at the _____?

4. A: This sweater is too big. I need to take it back to the store and <u>trade it</u> for

   a smaller one.

   B: Does that store let you _____ things?

Now change roles.

5. A: I hear you bought a new car. Did you <u>pay a fair price</u> for it?

   B: Yeah, I got _____ on it. My friend bought the same car but paid $1,000 more than I did.

6. A: Do you want to go shopping? I need to get some <u>things</u> for my apartment.

   B: No, thanks. I already have too much _____.

7. A: Are you going to buy that TV or are you going to <u>look at some other ones</u> first?

   B: I think I'll go to another store to _____ the prices.

8. A: I need to buy a birthday gift for my mother. This year I want to get something really <u>different</u>.

   B: Have you tried shopping on the Internet? I know a Website where you can buy _____ things.

9. A: I wish I knew how to do something <u>useful</u>, like fixing cars.

   B: Yeah, you're right. Fixing cars is a _____ skill.

2 *Work in a small group. Take turns asking the questions. Each student in the group answers the questions. Use the underlined words in your answers.*

1. Have you ever <u>exchanged</u> something? If so, what did you exchange? Why did you exchange it?

2. Do you like to <u>compare</u> prices from different stores before buying something? Why or why not?

3. Name something you bought that you got <u>a good deal</u> on. Where did you get it? Why do you think it was a good deal?

4. Do you have a lot of <u>stuff</u> in your house? What do you usually do with stuff that you don't use anymore—do you prefer to keep it, throw it away, or give it to someone else?

5. Name something you own that was <u>cheap</u> to buy. How much did it cost?

6. Do you usually buy things at the <u>regular price</u> or <u>on sale</u>? Why?

7. Describe something you own or something you can do that is <u>unusual</u>. What is unusual about it?

8. Do you like to buy things <u>used</u>? Why or why not? If yes, what are some things that you like to buy used? What are some things you never buy used?

9. Imagine you are in a barter network. What <u>skills</u> do you have? What's the most <u>valuable service</u> you can provide?

4 Focus on Speaking

A PRONUNCIATION: Numbers and Prices

When we say the numbers 13 through 19, *-teen* is stressed and the letter *t* in *-teen* sounds like /t/. When we say the numbers 20, 30, 40, 50, 60, 70, 80, and 90, the first syllable is stressed and the letter *t* in *-ty* sounds like a "fast" /d/.

 Listen to these examples:

13	30
/thirteen/	/thirdy/

16	60
/sixteen/	/sixdy/

19	90
/nineteen/	/ninedy/

There are two ways to say prices.

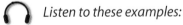 *Listen to these examples:*

$4.29   four dollars and twenty-nine cents
          four twenty-nine

$53.99   fifty-three dollars and ninety-nine cents
          fifty-three ninety-nine

1 *Listen to the numbers. Circle the number you hear.*

1. 13   30
2. 14   40
3. 15   50
4. 16   60
5. 17   70
6. 18   80
7. 19   90

2 *Work in pairs. Look at the numbers in Exercise 1 above. Take turns. Say a number. Remember to stress the correct syllable. Your partner points to the number you say.*

3 *Listen and write the prices you hear. Then practice saying them aloud in two different ways.*

1. $ _____

2. $ _____

3. $ _____

4. $ _____

5. $ _____

4 *Work in pairs. Take turns asking each other how much you usually spend on the following expenses. Write your partner's answers. Then compare your answers with the class.*

Example: A: How much do you usually spend on a haircut?

B: I spend thirty dollars. How about you?

A: I spend fifteen dollars.

1. a haircut $ _____

2. a movie ticket $ _____

3. your phone bill $ _____

4. a meal in a restaurant $ _____

B   STYLE: Negotiating—Making Suggestions and Coming to an Agreement

When two or more people need to make a decision together, they need to negotiate; they need to come to an agreement. When negotiating, you need to make suggestions until each person agrees.

Making Suggestions

Let's ...	buy this chair.
Why don't ...	we go to the thrift store?
How about ...	buying a used car instead of a new one?
	this one?
Would you like to ...	sell your computer?

Agreeing with Suggestions	**Disagreeing with Suggestions**
OK. / All right.	**Well, I don't know. How about ...?**
That's fine with me.	**I have another idea. Why don't we ...?**
That's a good idea.	**I don't think so.**
Let's do it.	
It's a deal.	
OK. Why not?	

1 *Look at the list of things below. Pretend you have $2,500 to buy things for your new house. Make a list of the things you would like to buy.*

used couch—$100	plants—$50
new couch—$700	pet kitten—$75
large armchair—$300	pet dog—$130
large floor rug—$200	computer—$800
lamp—$25	CD player—$250
bookcase—$115	television—$450
painting—$175	video-game player—$200

Your List

_____   _____   _____

_____   _____   _____

2 *Now work in a small group. Take turns suggesting things to buy. When everyone agrees, write your group's list below.*

Example: A: Let's buy the used couch for $100.

B: Well, I don't know. I don't want a used couch. How about buying the new one?

Your Group's List

_____   _____   _____

_____   _____   _____

3 *Share your group's list with another group. Explain why your group chose each thing. The other group listens and answers. Did you choose the same things? Why or why not?*

C   GRAMMAR: Comparative Adjectives

1 *Read the sentences. Notice the underlined words. Then answer the questions below.*

- I need to find a <u>cheaper</u> place to shop.

- The department store is <u>closer</u> than the outlet center.

a. What is the adjective in the first sentence? What does it describe? What two letters does the adjective end with?

b. What is the adjective in the second sentence? What does it describe? What word comes after *closer*?

Comparative Adjectives

1. Use the comparative form of the adjective to compare two people, places, or things. Use *than* before the second person, place, or thing.	This car is **cheaper** *than* that one. The new car is **more expensive** *than* the old one.
2. Add **-er** to form the comparative of short (one-syllable) adjectives.	cheap chea**per** old old**er**
Add **-r** if the adjective ends in **e**.	close close**r**
3. When a one-syllable adjective ends in a consonant + vowel + consonant, double the last consonant and add **-er.**	big big**ger** hot hot**ter**

(continued)

4. When two-syllable adjectives end in *-y,* change the *y* to *i* and add *-er.*

easy   eas**ier**
funny   funn**ier**

5. Some adjectives have irregular comparative forms.

good   **better**
bad   **worse**

6. To form the comparative of most adjectives of two or more syllables, add *more* before the adjective.

No service is *more* **valuable** than another one.

Less is the opposite of *more.*

Used clothing is *less* **expensive** than new clothing.

2 *Work in pairs. Look at the ads for the cars. Take turns making sentences comparing the two cars. Use the adjectives in the list on page 51. Then decide which car you would like to buy, and say why.*

Introducing the new

INDULGE

Buy a new *Indulge* and drive in comfort, style, and safety for only $40,000!

This week's special: a used

Pee Wee

This *Pee Wee* is old, but it runs well! It gets great gas mileage, and it's on sale now for only $1,000!

bad for the environment	expensive
big	good for a big family
cheap to drive	nice
comfortable	old
easy to park	safe

Example: A: The Indulge is bigger than the Pee Wee.

B: The Indulge is more expensive than the Pee Wee.

3 *Work in pairs. Write ten sentences comparing the Indulge and the Pee Wee. Read them out loud to the class.*

D SPEAKING TOPICS

Would you like to barter with your classmates? Follow these steps.

1. Get five blank cards. Write the following on each card:

a. name of an item you would like to exchange

b. how old it is

c. how much money you think it is worth now.

Example: computer
two years old
$300

2. Go around the class and barter with your classmates. Compare your items and negotiate until you come to an agreement. When you come to an agreement, trade your cards.

Example: A: How about trading your computer for my television?

B: But my computer is newer than your television.

A: Yeah, but my television is more valuable.

B: Thanks, but I want to keep looking. OR

B: OK. It's a deal.

3. Now report your exchanges to the class.

Example: A: I traded a three-year-old television worth $350 for a two-year-old computer worth $300.

B: That's a pretty good deal. Anything else?

Listening Task

Listen to your classmates' reports. Who made the most exchanges? Who got the best deal?

E RESEARCH TOPIC

Before most Americans buy something, especially something expensive, they do comparison shopping. They compare the different choices and then decide which is the best one to buy.

Practice comparison shopping for something you would like to buy. Follow these steps.

1. Think of something you would like to buy, such as a camera, a television, or a new jacket. Then go to a store and compare two different kinds. Or, go to two different stores to compare the prices on the same kind. Answer the following questions about your choice. Take notes.

   a. How much does it cost?

   b. What does it look like?

   c. How well is it made?

   d. How big is it?

   e. Is it what you need?

   f. Why is it better than the other one?

2. Report back to the class telling which item you would like to buy and why.

Listening Task

Listen to your classmates' reports and answer these questions.

1. Do you agree with the choice? Why or why not?

2. Which item would you like to buy?

For Unit 3 Internet activities, visit the NorthStar Companion Website at http://www.longman.com/northstar.

At Your Service: Service Animals

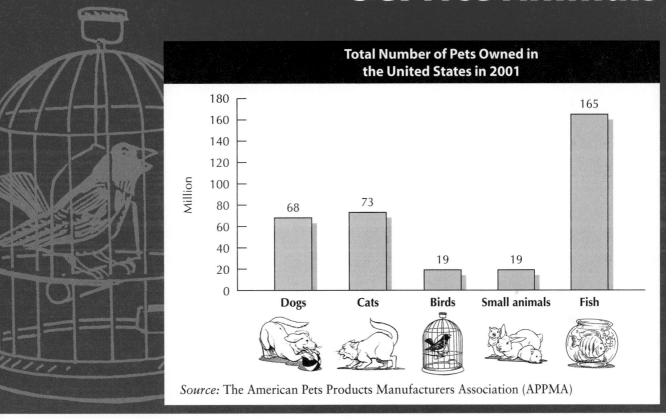

Total Number of Pets Owned in the United States in 2001

Source: The American Pets Products Manufacturers Association (APPMA)

1 Focus on the Topic

A PREDICTING

Look at the graph, and discuss these questions with the class.

1. Which pet was the most popular in 2001? Why do you think this pet was the most popular?

2. Why do people own these different pets?

3. Read the title of the unit. What do you think service animals are?

B   SHARING INFORMATION

1 Work in a group of four students. Write the names of the students in your group at the top of the chart. Discuss the questions in the chart. Write each student's answers.

Questions	_____ name	_____ name	_____ name	_____ name
1. Do you have any pets now? What kinds of pets do you have?				
2. Did you ever have pets? What kinds of pets did you have?				
3. What kinds of pets are popular in your home culture?				

2 Report your answers to the class.

Example: "In our group, three people have pets. One person doesn't have any pets."

3 Listen to all the reports. Then answer the following questions.

Which pets are the most popular? Why do you think they are so popular?

C   PREPARING TO LISTEN

BACKGROUND

1 Take this short quiz. Read each statement and check (✓) **True** or **False**.

	True	False
1. Dogs can help blind people.	❑	❑
2. Dogs can work in hospitals.	❑	❑
3. Dogs can be used to help sick people feel better.	❑	❑
4. Dogs can help people get dressed.	❑	❑

2 *Read this paragraph. Then answer the questions below. Share your answers with the class.*

Maybe you have seen blind people using a dog to help lead them. These are called Seeing Eye® dogs. They have been used for a very long time. Nowadays, trained dogs are used in many other ways. Some hospitals use "therapy dogs" to help patients feel better. Therapy dogs are companions to sick people, and studies have shown they help people feel better by reducing stress.

Other dogs can pick up keys a person dropped, open or close doors, help a person in and out of a bathtub, help drive a car, and even take off shoes, socks, and jackets. These dogs are called assistance or service dogs. Assistance dogs were first used about 25 years ago.

1. How did you do on the quiz? How many of your answers were correct?

2. What did you learn about dogs?

VOCABULARY FOR COMPREHENSION

Read these paragraphs. Then match each underlined word with the correct definition below. Write the number of the word next to the definition.

Many people have dogs as pets. Dogs can be friends to their (1) <u>owners</u>. They like to be with their owners and follow them around. Some dogs are more than pets; they are service dogs. Service dogs can (2) <u>assist</u> their owners in different ways. For example, some service dogs assist owners who can't see. They help their owners cross the street and get from place to place. Some service dogs assist people who are (3) <u>deaf</u>. These dogs are called (4) <u>hearing dogs</u>. Hearing dogs hear (5) <u>sounds</u> such as (6) <u>alarms</u>. Alarms ring to tell people there is an emergency, but deaf people can't hear the alarms. The hearing dogs tell deaf people about sounds by (7) <u>getting their attention</u>. Hearing dogs must make deaf people look at them. To get someone's attention, they touch the person.

Service dogs go to special schools and are (8) <u>trained</u> to help people. By assisting their owners, service dogs help their owners feel (9) <u>safe</u>. In fact, in emergencies, service dogs can really (10) <u>save someone's life</u>. They can protect a person from danger.

_____ **a.** things you hear   _____ **f.** making a person look at you

_____ **b.** dogs that assist deaf people   _____ **g.** protect someone from danger

_____ **c.** taught   _____ **h.** help

_1_ **d.** people who have something   _____ **i.** not hurt or in danger

_____ **e.** noises made in emergencies   _____ **j.** can't hear

2 Focus on Listening

A LISTENING ONE: *Kimba, the Hero Dog*

 Listen to the first part of "Kimba, the Hero Dog." Then read each question and circle the correct answer.

1. What are you listening to?
   a. a telephone message
   b. a news report
   c. an interview conversation

2. Where is the woman who is speaking?
   a. at a fire
   b. in the newsroom
   c. at her house

3. What do you think she is going to talk about? (*Circle more than one answer.*)
   a. people and dogs in general
   b. fires and dogs
   c. a special dog that helped someone
   d. the fire department
   e. the food dogs eat
   f. how dogs help people

LISTENING FOR MAIN IDEAS

 Listen to the complete news report. Which of the following questions are answered? Check (✓) the ones you hear.

_____ 1. What happened at the fire?

_____ 2. How do firefighters put out fires?

_____ 3. What do hearing dogs do?

_____ 4. How do people hear?

_____ 5. Why do people use hearing dogs?

_____ 6. What kind of fire alarms should people use?

_____ 7. How do hearing dogs tell deaf people about sounds?

_____ 8. What kind of dogs become hearing dogs?

_____ 9. Where do deaf people use hearing dogs?

_____ 10. How do people become deaf?

LISTENING FOR DETAILS

*Listen to the complete news report again. Then read each statement and decide if it is true or false. Write **T** (true) or **F** (false) next to it.*

_____ **1.** Mrs. Ravenscroft's dog, Kimba, is deaf.

_____ **2.** The fire started in the living room.

_____ **3.** Mrs. Ravenscroft saved Kimba's life.

_____ **4.** Hearing dogs tell deaf people about many sounds.

_____ **5.** First, the hearing dog goes to the deaf person and then to the sound.

_____ **6.** Hearing dogs cannot go into restaurants and stores.

_____ **7.** Hearing dogs are also companions.

_____ **8.** After the fire, Mrs. Ravenscroft called Kimba her personal hero dog.

Now go back to Section 2A (question 3) on page 56. Were your predictions correct?

REACTING TO THE LISTENING

1 *Listen to two excerpts from the news report. After listening to each excerpt, read the first question and circle the correct answer. Then answer the following questions. Discuss your answers with the class.*

Excerpt One

1. What do you think Steve is thinking?

    a. Wow! This is interesting.   **b.** I knew that.

2. What does he say to make you think that?

Excerpt Two

1. What do you think Steve is thinking?

    a. I didn't know that.   **b.** Everyone knows that.

2. What does he say to make you think that?

2 *Read this excerpt. Then discuss the questions below with the class. Give your opinions.*

". . . deaf people bring their dogs with them everywhere they go. Also, hearing dogs can go into all public places, such as restaurants and stores. Basically, a hearing dog can go to work, on the bus, and out to dinner, too!"

1. How do you feel about dogs going into restaurants and stores?

2. How do you feel about dogs going to work with their owners? Is this different from a restaurant or store? Why?

B LISTENING TWO: *Do People Help Animals, Too?*

1 *Describe the picture with your class. What do you see?*

2 *Work with a partner. Before you listen to "Do People Help Animals, Too?" look at the picture again. Then read the questions in the chart and write short answers in the "Before you listen" column.*

Questions	Before you listen	After you listen
1. Where is the dog?		
2. Who are the people standing on the street?		
3. Why is the truck there?		

3 *Now listen to the conversation. Then read the questions in the chart again. Write your answers in the "After you listen" column. Compare your "before" and "after" answers. Were your "before" answers correct?*

4 *Listen again to the conversation and answer these questions with your partner.*

1. How does the woman feel about saving the dog? How does the man feel?

2. Who do you agree with, the man or the woman? Why?

C   LINKING LISTENINGS ONE AND TWO

In Listenings One and Two, you heard about what animals do for people, and what people do for animals. Animals, service animals, or pets are treated differently all over the world.

Work in a small group. Look at the chart below. It lists some comments people make about their animals. Discuss each comment. Answer the questions. Use the words in the box to help you.

assistance	love	take care
companionship	safety	work

Comments	What does the animal do for the person or the person for the animal?	Do people in your country say things like this? If so, who?	What do you think about this comment?
1. "My cat is like a child to me."			
2. "I let my pets sleep on the bed with me."			
3. "My service animal changed my life."			
4. "When my pets are sick, I will spend as much money as necessary to make them better."			

3 Focus on Vocabulary

1 *Work in pairs. Look at the statements. The underlined words and phrases are used incorrectly. Student A, read a statement out loud. Student B, point out the incorrect word or phrase, why it is incorrect, and how to correct it. Use the words and phrases in the box below. Take turns reading the statements.*

caught on fire	hero	saves
companion	owns	service animals
get my attention	safe	trained

Example: A: Some animals are taught to do work for people. They are called <u>pets</u>.

B: The word "pets" is incorrect. Pets don't do work for people. The correct phrase is <u>service animals</u>.

A: That's right.

B: Kimba did a wonderful thing . . .

1. Kimba did a wonderful thing by saving Mrs. Ravenscroft's life. Kimba is a <u>bad dog</u>.

2. Kimba goes everywhere with Mrs. Ravenscroft. Kimba is Mrs. Ravenscroft's <u>house dog</u>.

3. Mrs. Ravenscroft knows Kimba will help her hear alarms. She feels <u>scared</u>.

4. It's amazing all the things dogs can do: Help people get dressed, open and close doors. They have to learn so much. I wonder how they are <u>fed</u>.

5. In the morning, my cat is always very hungry. She jumps on the bed and makes noise until I feed her. She tries to <u>be quiet</u>.

6. My mother loves birds. She has about five different kinds. They are beautiful to look at and they sing too. I am happy my mother <u>needs</u> birds so I can enjoy them too!

7. Some organizations find lost animals. If they are sick, the organization helps them get better. If the organization didn't take care of the animals, they'd die. The organization <u>buys</u> the animals.

8. There was a terrible accident in my neighborhood. Someone left a cigarette burning and a fire started. The house <u>was dangerous</u>.

2 *Work in pairs. Student A, read your lines in the following conversation. Student B, respond to Student A. Make sure you use some of the words and phrases in the box below.*

caught on fire	hero	saves
companion	owns	service dog
got her attention	safe	trained

1. A: I read a story in the newspaper today about that woman who lives
      nearby. You know, she has a special dog that works for people.
   B: *Oh yes. She has a service dog.* _____

2. A: Right. Well, she was home and there was a fire at her house.
   B: _____

3. A: Yeah. But no one was hurt. Everyone got out of the house.
   B: _____

4. A: Do you know how her dog told her about the fire?
   B: _____

   A: Well, the dog ran back and forth to the kitchen. Then the woman looked
      and saw the fire.

Now change roles.

5. A: Someone really taught that dog well.
   B: _____

6. A: It's good she has a service dog.
   B: _____

7. A: That dog is really a good friend.
   B: _____

8. A: And the dog did a great thing! He protected her from danger.
   B: _____

9. A: He did a wonderful thing.
   B: _____

4 Focus on Speaking

A PRONUNCIATION: Intonation of *Wh-* Questions

Intonation is the music, melody, or song of your voice.

When we ask a *wh-* question, our voice drops, or gets lower, as we end the question. The voice is high on the word we highlight (the most important word) in the question and then falls to a low note.

 Listen to these examples:

What do (service) animals do?

What does a (hearing) dog do?

Where do hearing dogs (go?)

 1 *Listen to the questions. Circle the word where the voice is high. Draw an arrow after the circled word. The voice falls after the circled word.*

1. What do service animals do?

2. What do hearing dogs do?

3. Where do deaf people use hearing dogs?

4. Why do deaf people use hearing dogs?

5. What do you think about hearing dogs?

2 *Work in pairs. Student A, ask the questions from Exercise 1 using falling intonation. Student B, answer the questions using the information from Listening One. Then change roles.*

B STYLE: Asking for More Information

A good way to keep a conversation going is to ask follow-up questions. Follow-up questions give you more information.

1 *Read the conversation. The follow-up questions are underlined.*

A: Kimba is a hearing dog.

B: <u>What do hearing dogs do?</u>

A: Hearing dogs are specially trained to assist deaf people.

B: <u>How do hearing dogs assist deaf people?</u>

A: They tell deaf people about sounds.

B: <u>What sounds do they tell deaf people about?</u>

A: They tell them about sounds like alarm clocks and ringing doorbells.

B: <u>Where do deaf people use their hearing dogs?</u>

A: Deaf people bring their dogs with them everywhere they go.

2 *Read each statment by A. Circle the appropriate follow-up question by B. (Read the whole conversation first, so you know which question makes sense.) Then practice the conversation out loud with a partner.*

1. A: I have a pet.

   B: **a.** What pet do you have?

     b. Where do you live?

2. A: I have a cat.

   B: **a.** What is your cat's name?

     b. What pets do you like?

3. A: Her name is Blue.

   B: **a.** That's a nice name. Does she like to play?

     b. Do you like cats?

4. A: Oh, yes. She loves to play. She's a great companion, too.

   B: **a.** Where do you go with her?

     b. Why is she a good companion?

5. A: She follows me around.

   B: **a.** Where does she follow you?

     b. Why do you have a cat?

6. A: She follows me into the garden.

   B: **a.** Where is your garden?

     b. What does she do?

   A: Oh, she sits and watches me water the flowers. Sometimes, she rubs up against me. Sometimes she makes noise to get my attention.

C   GRAMMAR: Simple Present Tense—*Wh-* Questions with *Do*

1 *Read the examples. Then answer the questions below.*

- What does a hearing dog do?

- Where do hearing dogs get their training?

- Why do people use hearing dogs?

a. What is the first word in each sentence? What kind of answer do you expect?

b. Underline the verbs. How many verbs are there in each sentence? What's the verb that is used in all three questions?

Wh- Questions with *Do*

1. *Wh-* questions ask for **information.** They cannot be answered by *yes* or *no. Wh-* questions start with a *wh-* word like **who, what, where, when,** and **why.**

A: **What** do hearing dogs do?
B: They help deaf people.
A: **Where** do they get their training?
B: They go to special schools.

2. To form most *wh-* questions in the simple present tense, use **do** or **does** and the base form of the verb.
Note that with the verb **be,** you do not use *do* or *does.*

Why **do** people **use** hearing dogs?
When **does** she **need** the dog?

Where **is** the school for hearing dogs?

- Use **do** with *I, you*, and *they.*

Where **do I** take the dog?
Why **do you** own a cat?
When **do they** use hearing dogs?

- Use **does** with *he, she,* or *it.*

Why **does he** own a hearing dog?
Who **does she** call for help?
When **does it** go to the door?

2 *Read the information about Canine* Companions for Independence (CCI) on page 65. CCI is an organization that trains service dogs.*

---

* *canine:* related to dogs

Canine Companions for Independence (CCI):

- non-profit organization
- five training centers in the United States
- gives dogs to people who need assistance in all states in the United States
- trains service dogs

Dogs

Hearing dogs for deaf people
- to tell deaf people about sounds

Service dogs for people with a physical disability
- to help open/close doors, turn lights on and off, pick up things from the floor
- to help people be more independent

Facility dogs for work with health professionals (physical therapists, caregivers)
- to help physical therapists teach patients to throw a ball as an exercise

Training
Puppies live with trainers until they are 15 months old
- trainers teach basic behavior

After 15 months old, dogs come to CCI for training
- training is six to eight months

Service
After training dogs, CCI gives them to people who need assistance
- person and dog take a two-week class together

Retirement
Service dogs retire after eight years and become regular pets

---

3 *Work in pairs. Take turns asking and answering questions about CCI. To answer the questions, look at the above information.*

Example: *Where / CCI have training centers?*

A: Where does CCI have training centers?

B: CCI has training centers in the United States.

1. Where / puppies live?
2. What / puppy trainers do?
3. What / service dogs do?
4. What / facility dogs do?
5. What / CCI do?
6. When / puppies start training?
7. When / people get service dogs?
8. When / service dogs retire?
9. Who / CCI give dogs to?
10. Why / puppy live with trainer?

D   SPEAKING TOPICS

In this unit you learned about animals as pets and as service animals. But animals are also used for food, clothing, and science. Many people disagree about the different uses of animals.

Work in a group of four students. Pick one of the four topics for discussion on pages 66–67. Then follow these steps.

1. Read the example discussion question below. Then make *wh-* questions with all of the phrases listed for the topic you picked.

    Example: Why do people use animals for food?

2. Student A, read a question. Student B, answer the question. Student C, ask a follow-up question. Student D, answer the follow-up question and ask another question from the list. Continue around the group until all the questions have been asked.

    Example: A: Why do people use animals for food?

    B: People use animals for food because animals are nutritious.

    C: Aren't vegetables nutritious, too?

    D: Yes, they are. But people like to eat meat, too.

    Why do people use animals for clothing like shoes and coats?

3. When you finish your topic, you can go on and do another one.

Topic 1: Vegetarians and Vegans

Some people are vegetarians. They don't eat meat. Other people are vegans. They don't eat or use anything made of animals—this includes clothing and food.

1. Why
   - people use animals for food
   - people use animals for clothing like shoes and coats

2. What
   - vegetarians eat
   - vegans eat
   - vegans use for shoes or clothing

3. Why
   - you think some people are vegetarians
   - you think some people are vegans

Topic 2: Fur Coats

You are going shopping and you see people standing in front of the store with signs that say, *Don't buy from this store—they sell fur coats. Cruelty to animals!*

1. Why
- people make fur coats
- people own fur coats
- some people not like fur coats

2. What animals
- people use to make fur coats

3. What
- you think about fur coats

Topic 3: Animal Testing

Often scientists use animals to test new medicines. They want to know if the medicine is safe for people to use. Also, companies that manufacture makeup or other health and beauty products use animals to test the products to see if they are safe for people. This is called animal testing.

1. Why
- people use animals to test products
- people not like animal testing

2. What
- scientists do during animal testing

3. Where
- animals that are used for testing live

4. What
- you think about animal testing

Topic 4: Pets

Pets are popular in the United States. Many people let their pets live in the house and even sleep on the bed. They treat their pets like children. When the pets are sick, people spend a lot of money to make them healthy again.

1. Where
- pets live in your country

2. What
- people in your country do with sick animals

3. Why
- people spend money to help a sick pet

4. What
- you think about pets sleeping on the bed
- you think about spending a lot of money to help a sick pet

E   RESEARCH TOPIC

You're going to interview a friend, neighbor, or teacher on the subject of service animals and pets. Follow these steps.

1. First, tell them what service animals do—work for people, work in hospitals, or provide companionship.

2. Then ask them their opinion about service animals and pets. Ask the questions below. Also, be sure to ask follow-up questions. Take notes.

   a. What do you think about service animals like hearing dogs or Seeing Eye® Dogs?

   b. What do you think about service animals in stores and restaurants?

   c. What do you think about facility dogs in hospitals?

   d. What pets do you like?

   e. Do you own pets? If so, what pets do you own?

   f. Where do you think pets should live, indoors or outdoors?

   g. How do you think pets can help people?

   h. Why do you think people like pets? Why do people dislike pets?

3. Work in a group of three students. Give a short report about your interview.

Listening Task

Listen to your classmates' reports. Compare their answers with your answers. Are they similar or different? What is similar? What is different?

For Unit 4 Internet activities, visit the NorthStar Companion Website at http://www.longman.com/northstar.

"Celletiquette"

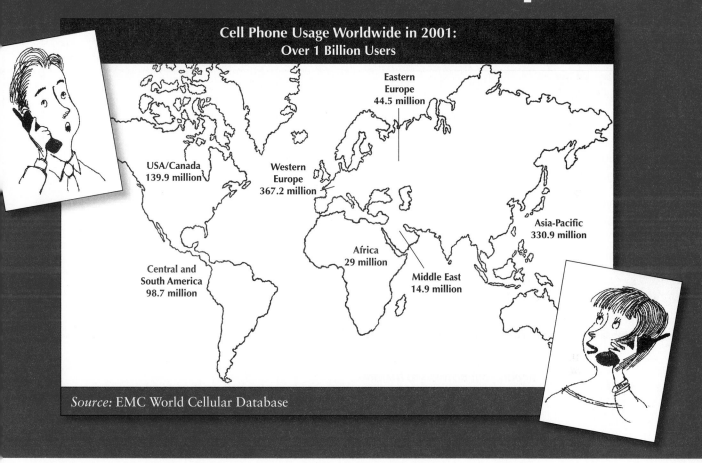

**Cell Phone Usage Worldwide in 2001:
Over 1 Billion Users**

Eastern
Europe
44.5 million

USA/Canada
139.9 million

Western
Europe
367.2 million

Asia-Pacific
330.9 million

Africa
29 million

Central and
South America
98.7 million

Middle East
14.9 million

Source: EMC World Cellular Database

1 Focus on the Topic

A PREDICTING

Look at the map, and discuss these questions with the class.

1. Which part of the world has the most cell phone users?

2. Are you surprised by these numbers? Why or why not?

3. Read the title of the unit. What do you think it means?

B   SHARING INFORMATION

1 *Work in a group of four students. Write the names of the students in your group at the top of the chart. Discuss the questions in the chart. Write each student's answers.*

Questions	name	name	name	name
1. Do you have a cell phone?				
2. If you have a cell phone, why do you have a cell phone?				
3. If you have a cell phone, how many times a day do you use it?				
4. Why do you think most people have cell phones?				

2 *Report your answers to the class.*

Example: In our group, two people have cell phones.

3 *Listen to all the groups' reports. Then answer the following questions.*

   1. How many students in the class have cell phones?

   2. What is the most popular reason to have a cell phone?

C   PREPARING TO LISTEN

BACKGROUND

Look at the results of a survey of Americans and cell phone use. These are some opinions North Americans have about cell phone usage.

1. What Is Your Attitude about Cell Phones?

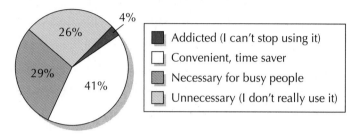

- ■ Addicted (I can't stop using it)
- □ Convenient, time saver
- ▨ Necessary for busy people
- ▨ Unnecessary (I don't really use it)

2. Where Should Cell Phones Be Banned?

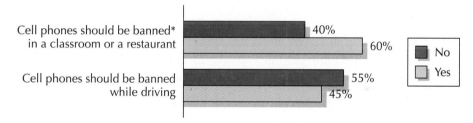

Cell phones should be banned* in a classroom or a restaurant — 40% / 60%

Cell phones should be banned while driving — 55% / 45%

■ No   ▨ Yes

Source: LetsTalk.com, "Cell Phone Bill of Rights, 2000."

Look at the above graphs. Discuss these questions with a partner.

Graph 1

1. What is the main reason Americans give for using a cell phone?

2. What do you think "necessary" means?

3. Why do people think cell phones are convenient?

Graph 2

1. What do many Americans think about cell phones and driving?

2. What do they think about cell phones in public places?

---

* *banned:* not allowed

VOCABULARY FOR COMPREHENSION

Read each statement. Then circle the correct definition of the underlined word(s).

1. Many people own cell phones and use them everyday. They keep their cell phone with them so it's easy to find, and they don't have to look for a pay phone. It is very <u>convenient</u>.

   a. easy to use   **b.** cheaper than a pay phone

2. I went to the movies last night. The people behind me talked the whole time, so I could not enjoy the movie. Their behavior was very <u>rude</u>.

   a. not polite   **b.** not quiet

3. To enjoy a movie, people want to see it and hear it, too. Everyone agrees it is not polite to talk during a movie. It is <u>common courtesy</u> to be quiet while watching a movie.

   a. the correct thing to do   **b.** the usual thing to do

4. When you are driving, it is important to <u>pay attention</u>. This means you need to look at the road and watch for other cars.

   a. concentrate on what you are doing   **b.** relax

5. People like to do many things while they are driving, for example, listen to the radio, eat, have conversations, and talk on the cell phone. These activities can be very <u>distracting</u>. They prevent people from concentrating on driving.

   a. making it easy to concentrate   **b.** making it difficult to concentrate

6. Anyone with a license has the <u>right</u> to drive; no one can tell them not to.

   a. agree to do something   **b.** permission to do something

7. There are <u>laws</u> people must follow while driving. If you do not follow them, you can get a ticket.

   a. rules   **b.** tickets

8. Now that more and more people have cell phones, you can <u>overhear</u> many conversations. You can hear people talking—but they are not talking to you.

   a. hear someone talking to you   **b.** hear someone talking to another person

9. Some conversations are <u>private</u>, for example, I heard one woman having an argument with her husband.

   a. for everybody in general   **b.** for some people only

10. I heard a woman having an argument with her husband on the phone. She was sitting in the park, which is a very <u>public place</u> and there were many people around.

    a. a place anyone may go   **b.** a place not open for everybody

2 Focus on Listening

A LISTENING ONE: *Everyone Has an Opinion*

 Listen to the beginning of "Terry Talks to the Town." Then read each question and circle the correct answer.

1. What are you listening to?
   a. a TV talk show
   b. a radio call in show
   c. an interview

2. What is the topic of the show?
   a. Do you have a cell phone?
   b. What do you think about cell phones?
   c. Do you have a problem with your cell phone?

3. What do you think people will say? (*Write three ideas.*)

   _____

   _____

   _____

LISTENING FOR MAIN IDEAS

 *Listen to the people calling the "Terry Talks to the Town" show to give their opinions on the subject of cell phones. Are these callers **pro** (for) or **con** (against) cell phones? Circle the correct word.*

Caller	Opinion
1	pro con
2	pro con
3	pro con
4	pro con
5	pro con

LISTENING FOR DETAILS

 Listen to the complete "Terry Talks to the Town" show again. Check (✓) the correct information about each caller. What is his or her opinion or complaint? You can check (✓) more than one answer for each caller.

Caller	What is his or her opinion or complaint?
1	_____ **a.** distracting
	_____ **b.** people should be careful
	_____ **c.** convenient, saves time
	_____ **d.** good for safety
	_____ **e.** my right to use a cell phone
2	_____ **a.** distracting
	_____ **b.** people should be careful
	_____ **c.** people should be responsible
	_____ **d.** rude in public places
	_____ **e.** people need common courtesy
3	_____ **a.** distracting
	_____ **b.** rude in public places
	_____ **c.** my right to use a cell phone
	_____ **d.** people need common courtesy
	_____ **e.** people need to be careful
4	_____ **a.** people should be careful
	_____ **b.** convenient, saves time
	_____ **c.** good for safety
	_____ **d.** my right to use a cell phone
	_____ **e.** people need to be careful
5	_____ **a.** convenient, saves time
	_____ **b.** good for safety
	_____ **c.** my right to use a cell phone
	_____ **d.** people need common courtesy
	_____ **e.** people need to be careful

Now go back to Section 2A (question 3) on page 73. Were your predictions correct?

REACTING TO THE LISTENING

1 *Listen to two excerpts from the "Terry Talks to the Town" show. After listening to each excerpt, check (✓) the correct statement about Terry, and answer the following question. Discuss your answers with the class.*

Excerpt One

1. _____ Terry thinks talking and driving is a good idea.

   _____ Terry doesn't think talking and driving is a good idea.

2. How do you know?

Excerpt Two

1. _____ Terry thinks people should be able to talk on the phone in restaurants.

   _____ Terry doesn't think people should talk on the phone in restaurants.

2. How do you know?

2 *What do you think about cell phones? Answer the following questions. Then discuss your answers with two other students. Give your opinions.*

1. Where do you think cell phones should be allowed? Write **Yes** next to the places. Where should people not use cell phones? Write **No** next to those places. (Sometimes people use cell phones in emergency situations. Imagine these are not emergencies.)

   _____ movie theaters   _____ on buses

   _____ restaurants   _____ in school

   _____ while driving   _____ in other public places

2. Which reasons do you think are good reasons to use a cell phone? Check (✓) three.

   _____ safety

   _____ convenience

   _____ saves time

   _____ I like it

   _____ business

   _____ emergencies

B   LISTENING TWO: *Our Listeners Write*

 Listen to Terry read three e-mails from his listeners. They are giving him suggestions on how to control rude cell phone behavior. Then read each sentence. Circle the answer that completes the sentence.

E-mail One

1. The listener suggests a device called a _____.

   a. blocking device   **b.** jamming device   **c.** cell phone signal

2. The device _____ cell phone signals.

   a. turns off   **b.** blocks   **c.** controls

E-mail Two

1. The listener thinks restaurants should _____.

   a. not control people's   **b.** put up signs   **c.** be quiet
   behavior

2. The listener suggests _____.

   a. using "quiet cars"   **b.** having laws   **c.** putting up a sign
   on trains

E-mail Three

1. The listener thinks we need _____ about cell phones and driving.

   a. signs   **b.** behavior   **c.** laws

2. The listener thinks people can't _____.

   a. control their behavior   **b.** drive safely   **c.** be polite

C   LINKING LISTENINGS ONE AND TWO

Use what you learned from Listenings One and Two. Complete the chart below with what you think is the best solution for each problem. Then work with three other students. Compare and discuss your solutions.

Problem	Solution
1. Using cell phones while driving	
2. Using cell phones in restaurants	
3. Using cell phones in movie theaters	

3 Focus on Vocabulary

1 *Work in pairs. Student A, look at this page. Student B, look at page 163. Follow the instructions there.*

Student A, you and Student B each have a crossword puzzle. You each have four words filled in. You each are missing four words. To complete the crossword puzzle, you need to know the words your partner has, and your partner needs to know the words you have. Take turns reading the clues. For each clue, tell your partner the number and if it is across or down. Your partner will try to guess the word. Tell your partner if he or she is correct. When you guess the correct word, write it into the crossword puzzle.

Student A, read these clues to your partner. Student B will try to guess the word. If B is correct, say, "That's correct." If B made a mistake, say, "That's not correct."

1. *(across)* One caller said this is why he uses a cell phone while driving. Another way to say it is "use less time." *(2 words)*

3. *(across)* One caller complained about cell phones in public places. Another way to say this is "to interrupt or annoy someone."

5. *(across)* Some countries allow jamming devices. In these countries, they are "allowed by law."

7. *(across)* This word describes someone who is not polite.

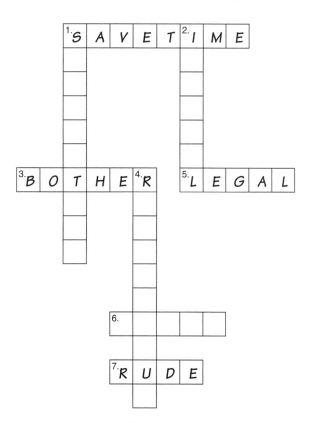

Student A, now listen to the clues read by Student B and try to guess the words. Use the following list to help you. When you have guessed correctly, write the word in your crossword puzzle.

block	illegal	ridiculous	save time
bother	legal	rude	suggestion

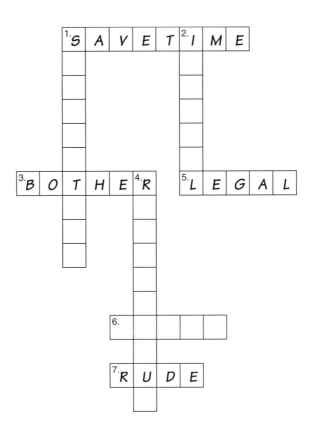

2 *Work in a small group. Take turns asking the questions. Each student in the group answers the questions. Use the underlined words in your answers.*

1. How do you <u>save time</u>?

2. Talk about something that <u>bothers</u> you. Why does it bother you?

3. Talk about a time someone did something <u>rude</u>. Why did you think it was rude?

4. What is the best <u>suggestion</u> you have ever made?

5. What is the most <u>ridiculous</u> thing you have ever seen?

6. Have you ever <u>overheard</u> a conversation? What did you hear?

7. What is something that is very <u>distracting</u> for you?

8. Do you own something that makes your life <u>convenient</u>? What is it and how does it make your life convenient?

4 Focus on Speaking

A   PRONUNCIATION: Unstressed *to*

When we use *to* in sentences, we do not stress it. Before words beginning with consonants, we often pronounce it like a strong "t."

Listen to the way **to** *sounds:*

> I hate to leave.
> And I'd love to stay.
> But I have to go.

1 *Listen to the way* **to** *sounds in this chant. Repeat the lines. Then practice the chant with a partner.*

> I'm going to call you on my cell phone
> to see what you want to do
> to make a plan
> for later on
> to meet and visit with you
> we can meet to go to the store
> or meet to see a movie
> or meet to hang out and talk
> and just spend a nice day together!

2 *Work in pairs. Student A uses a cell phone all the time. Student B thinks most cell phone users are rude. Listen to each pair of statements. Which statement would Student A make? Which statement would Student B make? Check (✓)* **Student A** *or* **Student B.** *Then read these statements out loud.*

	Student A	Student B
1. **a.** I have a right to use my cell phone.	❑	❑
b. I have the right to watch the movie in peace.	❑	❑
2. **a.** I hate to listen to your private conversations.	❑	❑
b. I hate to use pay phones. They are too expensive.	❑	❑
3. **a.** I like to talk to my friends on the phone all day.	❑	❑
b. I like to talk to my friends in a restaurant.	❑	❑
4. **a.** I like to drive and talk on the phone; it saves time.	❑	❑
b. I like to feel safe when I drive. I like to know all drivers are watching the road!	❑	❑

B STYLE: Expressing Likes and Dislikes

There are different ways to express likes and dislikes.

Expressing Likes	Expressing Dislikes
How do you like your cell phone?	How do you like hearing other people's cell phones?
It's **great!**	It **bothers** me
I **love** it.	I **don't like** it.
I **really like** it.	I **can't stand** it.
I **like** it.	I **hate** it.
I **don't mind** it.	

Fluency Line

Work in two groups, A and B. Each group stands in a line so that Group A students are standing opposite Group B students. You will all be talking at the same time. Then you will switch to a new partner. You will all need to use your books.

Students in Group A will begin. Ask your partners (standing opposite you in Group B) the questions below. Your partners respond using one of the expressions above. Continue asking the questions and answering them until your teacher tells you to switch. When your teacher says, "Switch," students in Group A move to the next partner. Students in Group B stay in one place.

1. How do you like cell phones?

2. How do you like people using cell phones in public places?

3. How do you like talking on a cell phone while driving?

4. How do you like the idea of laws against cell phones?

5. How do you like the idea of "quiet cars"?

6. How do you like the idea of jamming devices?

Talking on a cell phone while driving

C   GRAMMAR: Verbs Plus Gerunds and Infinitives

1 *Read the sentences. Notice the underlined words. Then answer the questions.*

- I <u>like using</u> a cell phone.

  I <u>like to use</u> a cell phone.

- I <u>want to have</u> a private conversation.

  I <u>don't want to overhear</u> private conversations.

- We <u>enjoy learning</u> about new technology.

a. What are the verbs? Circle them.

b. What words follow *like*? *want*? *enjoy*?

c. How are the words after *like*, *want*, and *enjoy* different?

Verbs Plus Gerunds and Infinitives

1. Some verbs can be followed by a **gerund** (base form of a verb + *-ing*). For example, *enjoy, keep,* and *dislike*.

I *enjoy* **talking** on my cell phone.
I *don't enjoy* **talking** on my cell phone.
He *keeps* **using** his cell phone in public.

2. Some verbs can be followed by an **infinitive** (*to* + base form of the verb). For example, *want, need, ask, agree,* and *promise*.

We *want* **to buy** a hands-free device.
I *don't want* **to hear** cell phones ringing.
People *need* **to be** more careful.

3. Some verbs can be followed by **a gerund or an infinitive.** For example, *like, love, hate,* and *prefer*.

I *like* **using** cell phones.
I *like* **to use** cell phones.
I *love* **having** a cell phone.
I *love* **to have** a cell phone.

---

2 *Work in a group of three students. Read the sentences. Complete each sentence. Use the gerund or infinitive of the verb in parentheses.*

1. She asked _____ the work later.
$\qquad$ (do)

2. I love _____ on a cell phone.
$\qquad$ (talk)

3. He keeps _____ his phone.
$\qquad$ (answer)

4. I hate _____ private conversations.
$\qquad$ (overhear)

5. I agreed _____ my cell phone in public places.
$\qquad$ (turn off)

6. We promise _____ home by 8:00.
(come)

7. I enjoy _____ a movie in a quiet theater.
(watch)

8. They need _____ their cell phones for work.
(use)

9. Some people don't want _____ common courtesy.
(use)

10. Many people don't like _____ laws about cell phones.
(have)

3 *Interview three students in your class. Write their names at the top of the chart below. Choose four of the following questions and write them in the chart. Then ask your questions to the three students and write their answers. When everyone is done, discuss the answers with the class.*

Why do you think people . . .

> own cell phones?
> like cell phones?
> don't like cell phones?
> talk and drive or don't talk and drive?
> want laws or don't want laws?
> hate to hear cell phones ringing?
> don't like to overhear private conversations?

Example: A: Why do you think people talk on the phone and drive?

B: They want to save time.

Questions	_____ name	_____ name	_____ name
1.			
2.			
3.			
4.			

D SPEAKING TOPICS

You're going to do a role play with a partner. Follow these steps.

1. Read the example situation and practice the example role play.

Example Situation

Student A and Student B are on a bus. They are sitting together, but they don't know each other. B is reading a book. A's cell phone rings.

Student A, you answer the phone and start talking very loudly to your girlfriend. She wants you to go shopping for dinner. Student B, you're trying to read a book for school, but you can't because you're overhearing A's conversation.

Example Role Play

A: Hello . . . Yeah . . . (*loudly*) Hi! I'm on Fourth and Mission.

B: Excuse me . . . This is a bus. I want to read my book. I don't like overhearing your conversation. Can you talk later?

A: It'll only take a minute . . . OK. So I'll go shopping. What should I get?

B: Didn't you hear what I said? This is a public place . . . I don't want to listen to your conversation. Please turn off your phone or get off the bus.

2. Choose one of the situations below. Write a role play like the one in the example. Use some of the vocabulary, style, and grammar from this unit.

Situation 1

Student A and Student B are in a nice restaurant, having a quiet dinner together. A man at a nearby table starts a loud conversation on his cell phone. It sounds like he is breaking up with his girlfriend.

Student A, you want to discuss with B a problem you are having at work. You start talking about your problem, but B is listening to the man's conversation. Student B, you want to listen to your friend's problem, but the man's conversation sounds much more interesting and you listen to that instead.

Situation 2

Student A and Student B are in a park. It's Saturday morning.

Student A, had a very busy week and wants to relax and talk to B. Student B, you were too busy all week to return phone calls. You brought your cell phone to the park and start to make calls.

3. Perform your role play for the class.

Listening Task

Watch the role plays. Which role play did you like best? Discuss with a partner why you liked that role play.

E   RESEARCH TOPIC

A cell phone is a high-tech communication device. There are many other high-tech devices that people use every day to communicate. Some examples are:

a PDA (a Palm Pilot or a Visor Handspring)
a wireless device such as Blackberry
a laptop computer with a wireless modem
a two-way pager
a two-way radio

You're going to research a high-tech communication device. Follow these steps.

1. Go to a store that sells high-tech devices or look in a catalogue. Pick a high-tech communication device. Find out where it is used and who uses it. Think of three pros and cons for using the device. Fill in the information below.

   Name of the device: _____

   Where you found out about the device: _____

   How it works: _____

   Why people might use the device (pros): _____

   _____

   _____

   Problems you can imagine with high-tech etiquette (cons): _____

   _____

   _____

2. When you are done, tell the class about your device.

Listening Task

Listen to your classmates' reports. Which device sounds like something you might buy? Why? Pick two devices. Take notes. When all the reports are done, share your answers with a partner.

 For Unit 5 Internet activities, visit the NorthStar Companion Website at http//www.longman.com/northstar.

Is It Women's Work?

1 Focus on the Topic

A PREDICTING

Look at the picture, and discuss these questions with the class.

1. What activities do you see? Who is doing each activity? (*Point to the people in the picture.*)

2. Read the title of the unit. What do you think the unit will be about?

B   SHARING INFORMATION

Work in a group of four students. Write the names of the students at the top of the chart. Discuss who does the following chores in your home. Write each student's answers.

Chores in your home	_____ name	_____ name	_____ name	_____ name
1. Who does the cooking?				
2. Who does the cleaning?				
3. Who repairs things?				
4. Who takes care of the children?				

C   PREPARING TO LISTEN

BACKGROUND

1 *Read the information and look at the graph below.*

In 1948, only 32 percent of women in the United States worked. In 2001, 59 percent of American women had jobs.

Percentages of Male/Female Jobs in the United States (2001)

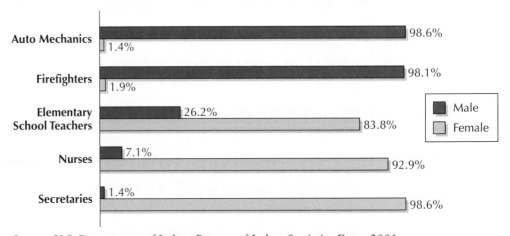

Source: U.S. Department of Labor, Bureau of Labor Statistics Data, 2001

2 *Work with a partner. Discuss the following questions. Then share your answers with the class.*

1. What percentage of American women worked in 2001? Why do you think more women are working now than they did in the past?

2. Which jobs are usually done by females? Why do you think women usually do those jobs?

3. Which jobs are usually done by males? Why do you think men usually do those jobs?

4. Do you think these percentages are about the same in your country? If not, which do you think are different? Why do you think so?

5. Do you think these percentages will change in the future? If so, how do you think they will change?

VOCABULARY FOR COMPREHENSION

Read these paragraphs. Then match each underlined word with the correct definition below. Write the number of the word next to the definition.

Families all over the world are different: There is no (1) <u>typical</u> family. In different families, men and women sometimes do different (2) <u>household chores</u> such as cooking and cleaning. But, there is one question all families with children have: Who takes care of the children when parents work? Who does the (3) <u>childcare</u>?

There are a few choices for working parents. One choice is to take the children to a day-care center. Parents can bring their children to the day-care center before work and pick them up after work. Another choice is to (4) <u>hire</u> a sitter whose job it is to take care of children. A sitter may take care of children in his or her house or come to the family's house. Still another choice is to hire a (5) <u>nanny</u>. A nanny usually lives with a family and takes care of the children. Sometimes (6) <u>childcare workers</u> go to school where they get (7) <u>training</u> in taking care of children.

_____ **a.** taking care of children while parents work

_____ **b.** give a job to

_____ **c.** education to learn how to do something

_____ **d.** work in the house such as cooking and cleaning

_____ **e.** people who take care of children

_____ **f.** a person who usually lives with a family and takes care of the children

_____ **g.** usual or regular

2 Focus on Listening

A   LISTENING ONE: *Who's Taking Care of the Children?*

 Listen to the beginning of a TV talk show. Then read each question and circle the correct answer.

1. What is the talk show about?
   a. men and women
   b. childcare
   c. children

2. Who is Julie Jones going to interview?
   a. a parent
   b. a nanny
   c. a young child

3. What are three questions you think Julie Jones will ask?

   a. _____

   b. _____

   c. _____

LISTENING FOR MAIN IDEAS

 Read this list of issues. Then listen to the whole TV talk show and put the issues in order from 1 to 4. (Which issue is discussed first, second, third, and so on.)

   _1_   a. childcare in the United States

   ____   b. what a nanny does

   ____   c. what one family thinks
            about male nannies

   ____   d. how this man became a
            nanny

LISTENING FOR DETAILS

 Listen to the TV talk show again. Read each pair of sentences. Circle the sentence that is true.

1. a. More than 50 percent of families with children in the United States pay for childcare.
   b. Fewer than 50 percent of families with children in the United States pay for childcare.

2. a. A woman is sometimes called a manny.
   b. A man is sometimes called a manny.

3. a. A male and female nanny do the same things.
   b. A male and female nanny do different things.

4. a. Less than 5 percent of nannies in the United States are men.
   b. Less than 15 percent of nannies in the United States are men.

5. a. This male nanny likes doing household chores.
   b. This male nanny doesn't like doing household chores.

6. a. This male nanny went to a special school that trains nannies.
   b. This male nanny didn't go to a special school that trains nannies.

7. a. It was easy for this male nanny to find work.
   b. It wasn't easy for this male nanny to find work.

8. a. The mother who hired this male nanny has two boys.
   b. The mother who hired this male nanny has two girls.

9. a. The children like having a male nanny.
   b. The children don't like having a male nanny.

10. a. At first, the husband liked the manny being alone with his wife.
   b. At first, the husband didn't like the manny being alone with his wife.

Now go back to Section 2A (question 3) on page 88. Were your predictions correct?

REACTING TO THE LISTENING

 Listen to three excerpts from the TV talk show. After listening to each excerpt, read the first question and circle the correct answer. Then answer the following questions.

Excerpt One

1. How does Julie Jones feel when she meets the nanny?

   a. She is surprised.   **b.** She is angry.

2. How do you know?

3. Why do you think she feels that way?

Excerpt Two

1. How does Julie Jones feel when the man says he likes household chores?

   a. She is surprised.   **b.** She is excited.

2. How do you know?

3. Why do you think she feels that way?

Excerpt Three

1. How does the man feel about the question?

    a. He is angry.   **b.** He is embarrassed.

2. How do you know?

3. Why do you think he feels that way?

2 *Discuss these questions with the class. Give your opinions.*

1. Think back to when you were a child. Who took care of you? Would you have liked to have a nanny? If yes, would you have liked a male or female nanny? Why?

2. Does your family use childcare now? If so, what kind of childcare do you use? What kind of childcare do you think is best?

B   LISTENING TWO: *Who Is Right for the Job?*

 1 *Listen to three conversations. The people are discussing men's and women's work. Draw a line from each conversation to the job discussed in that conversation.*

Conversation 1	auto mechanic
Conversation 2	firefighter
Conversation 3	elementary school teacher

 2 *Listen again. Who do the people in the conversations think can do the jobs they are discussing? Circle* **men, women,** *or* **both** *and write the reason.*

	Who can do the job?	Reason
Conversation 1 What does the man think?	men / women / both	
Conversation 2 What does the man think?	men / women / both	
Conversation 3 What does the woman think?	men / women / both	

C   LINKING LISTENINGS ONE AND TWO

In Listenings One and Two you heard about men and women doing different kinds of work. Who do YOU think is right for each job? Circle your answer and write why you think so. Then discuss your answers with the class.

Job	Who is right for the job?	Why do you think so?
Nanny	men / women / both	
Firefighter	men / women / both	
Elementary School Teacher	men / women / both	
Auto Mechanic	men / women / both	

3 Focus on Vocabulary

1 *Complete the conversations with words or phrases from the box. Use the underlined words to help you. Then work in pairs. Practice the conversations out loud with your partner. Change roles after item 4.*

be good at (something)	hire
break down	role model
get along	to tell you the truth
have a problem with (something)	typical

1. A: My son wants to be a nurse! Men don't <u>usually</u> work as nurses.

   B: You're right. That isn't a _____ job for a man.

2. A: I'm <u>not happy</u> that he wants to be a nurse. I think he should be a doctor.

   B: I disagree. I don't _____ that at all.

3. A: Jennifer <u>does well</u> in all of her classes. She got A's in math and English!

   B: Wow, she's lucky she _____ so many things.

4. A: Do you <u>have a good time</u> with your brothers and sisters?

   B: Yes, we all _____ very well.

Now change roles.

be good at (something)	hire
break down	role model
get along	to tell you the truth
have a problem with (something)	typical

5. A: I've been looking for work for a long time, but so far no one wants to <u>give me a job</u>.

   B: Really? Maybe my boss will _____ you.

6. A: I was driving home late last night and suddenly my car just <u>stopped running</u>!

   B: That happened last week, too. Your car _____ often.

7. A: I work hard and I try to be a good person, so I can set a good <u>example</u> for my kids.

   B: Good for you. Your kids are lucky to have a good _____.

8. A: What do <u>you really think</u> about male nannies?

   B: Well, _____, I don't think men should be nannies.

2 *Work in a small group. Take turns asking the questions. Each student in the group answers the questions. Use the underlined words in your answers.*

1. What are you <u>good at</u>?

2. What kind of person would you <u>hire</u> to take care of your children? Would you hire a man or a woman? a stranger or a relative? someone with or without training? someone who speaks your language?

3. Who do you think is a good <u>role model</u> for children? Why do you think he or she is a good role model?

4. Who do you <u>get along</u> with the best? Why do you get along so well?

5. What's a <u>typical</u> morning for you? What do you do?

6. Does your car ever <u>break down</u>? If so, what did you do the last time it broke down?

7. Name something you <u>have a problem with</u>. Why do you have a problem with it?

4 Focus on Speaking

A PRONUNCIATION: Intonation

Intonation is the rising and falling of your voice. In speaking, we use intonation
to change the meaning of a word. The same word with different intonation can
have different meanings.

 Listen to these examples of rising intonation:

- To show surprise:

  MAN: I enjoy doing housework.

  WOMAN: Really?

- To request more information:

  MAN: I was home alone with his wife.

  WOMAN: And? . . .

  MAN: Well, her husband was worried.

- To request repetition or clarification:

  WOMAN: I'm going to the post office now.

  MAN: Where?

  WOMAN: To the post office.

 Listen to these examples of falling intonation:

- To show disbelief:

  MAN: More men are working as nannies these days.

  WOMAN: Hmm . . .

- To show that you are thinking or are going to say more:

  WOMAN: Was it easy for you to find work as a nanny?

  MAN: Well . . .

1 Listen to the conversations. First, circle the best description of the person's response (**a.** or **b.**). Then draw an arrow above each response: —⟋ for rising intonation or ⌒ for falling intonation. Practice saying the words using the correct intonation.

1. Really.   (a.) The man is surprised.   b. The man doesn't believe it.

2. Really.   a. The woman is surprised.   b. The woman doesn't believe it.

3. Well . . .   a. The woman wants the man to say more.   b. The woman is going to say more.

4. Well . . .   a. The woman wants the man to say more.   b. The woman is going to say more.

5. Hmm . . .   a. The man is asking a question.   b. The man is thinking.

6. Hmm . . .   a. The man is asking a question.   b. The man is thinking.

2 Work in pairs. Student A, read each sentence. Student B, listen to Student A's sentence. Then respond according to the description in parentheses. Change roles after sentence 3.

Student A	**Student B**
1. I got an A on my English test.	Really . . . (*You are surprised.*)
2. When I was young, my father did all the housework.	You're kidding . . . (*You don't believe it.*)
3. I'll meet you at 6:00.	When . . . (*You didn't hear the time.*)
4. My sister is a firefighter.	A firefighter . . . (*You are surprised.*)
5. What do you think about mannies?	Well . . . (*You are thinking.*)
6. I just met my boyfriend's parents.	And . . . (*You want to hear more.*)

B   **STYLE: Expressing Opinions and Agreeing or Disagreeing**

Often in conversation, we want to express opinions on a topic. An opinion is something you believe to be true. Different people can have different opinions about the same thing. You can agree or disagree with an opinion. To get other people to agree with you, you should give reasons to support your opinion. You should say why you believe your opinion is true.

Expressing an Opinion		**Supporting your Opinion**
I think		
I feel	men and women should	**because** children can learn
I believe	share childcare	from both parents.
In my opinion,		
I don't think		
I don't feel	men and women should	**because** men are not very
I don't believe	share childcare	good at childcare.
In my opinion,	men and women should**n't**	
	share childcare.	

Agreeing with an Opinion	**Disagreeing with an Opinion**
I think so, too.	**I don't think so.**
I agree.	**I don't agree.**
	I disagree.

Work in a group of three students. Take turns reading one of the following statements. The other students either agree or disagree with the statement and give their opinion and a reason to support their opinion.

Example: A: Women are better at cooking than men.

B: I agree. I think women are better at cooking than men because women learn from their mothers.

C: I disagree. I don't think women are better at cooking than men because all the great chefs are men.

Statements

1. Women are better at cooking than men.
2. Men are better at repairing things than women.
3. Women should do all the cleaning in a house.
4. Women with young children shouldn't work outside the home.
5. Working women are good role models for their children.
6. Men should be responsible for all the money in a household.
7. Men should stay home and take care of children.

C   GRAMMAR: Adverbs and Expressions of Frequency

1 *Read the sentences. Notice the underlined words. Then answer the questions below.*

- A nanny <u>always</u> takes care of the children.

- A nanny <u>sometimes</u> cooks dinner for the children.

- A nanny is <u>usually</u> a woman.

a. What are the verbs? Circle them.

b. What question do the underlined words answer?

c. In which sentence does the underlined word appear after the verb? What's the verb?

d. In all three sentences, what tense are the verbs in? Why?

Adverbs and Expressions of Frequency

1. Some adverbs of frequency are:

always   *usually*   *often*   *sometimes*   *rarely*   *never*

2. Some expressions of frequency are:

every (day, week, month)   *twice (a week)*   *once in a while*
several times (a year)   *three times (a month)*

3. Use adverbs and expressions of frequency to tell how often someone does something.	I **usually** help Kate get ready for school. Her father drives her to school **every day.**
4. The verbs used with adverbs and expressions of frequency are usually in the simple present tense.	A nanny **always** *takes* care of the children. He *cooks* dinner **every night.**
5. Adverbs of frequency come after the verb *be.*	A nanny *is* **usually** a woman.
Adverbs of frequency usually come before other verbs.	Husbands **sometimes** *worry* about male nannies.
Sometimes can also come at the beginning of a sentence.	**Sometimes** husbands worry about male nannies.
6. Expressions of frequency usually come at the beginning or the end of the sentence.	I pick her up after school **every day. Once in a while,** we go to the movies.
7. Use *How often ...?* in questions about frequency.	**How often** do you go to the movies?

2 *Work in pairs. Take turns asking each other if you ever do one of the activities in the list below (or think of your own activities). When your partner answers "Yes," ask how often he or she does that activity. Ask each other six questions. Your answers must include an adverb or expression of frequency (see the list below). Write down your partner's answers.*

Example: A: Do you ever clean your house?

B: Yes, I do.

A: How often do you clean your house?

B: I clean my house once a week.

Activities	**Adverbs and Expressions of Frequency**
clean your house	once a day / week / month / year
dream in English	twice a day / week / month / year
eat dessert	three times a day / week / month / year
listen to the radio	every day / night / week / month / Sunday
pay bills	several times a week
take vacations	once in a while
talk to a good friend	rarely
think about someone special	never
think about the future	

D   SPEAKING TOPICS

Compare the roles of men and women in the United States with the roles of men and women in your home culture. Follow these steps.

1. Read the chart below. It gives information about men and women in the United States.

MALE/FEMALE JOBS IN THE UNITED STATES (2001)		
Jobs	**Male**	**Female**
Police Officers	85.8%	14.2%
Doctors	75.5%	24.5%
Judges and Lawyers	71%	29%
Cooks	56%	44%
Bookkeepers and Accounting Clerks	8.6%	91.4%

Source: U.S. Department of Labor, Bureau of Labor Statistics Data, 2001.

2. Now work in a group. Take turns making statements using the information in the chart. React to the information by talking about your home culture. Use adverbs of frequency. Then give your opinion about the information.

Example: A: About 14 percent of police officers in the United States are women. In my country, women rarely work as police officers.

B: In my country, it's the same. Women rarely work as police officers. In my opinion, women shouldn't work as police officers because police officers need to be strong, and the work is dangerous.

C: Really? I disagree . . .

E   RESEARCH TOPIC

In this unit, you learned about male nannies. Taking care of children is an unusual activity for a man. Find out other unusual jobs or activities for men and women. Follow these steps.

1. For one week, look around in the city or town where you live, and on TV. Notice the jobs or activities you see men and women doing. Which ones do you think are unusual for a man or a woman?

2. Write down unusual jobs or activities for each and the reason you think it's unusual.

Unusual Jobs / Activities for Men	**Reason I Think It's Unusual**
_____	_____
_____	_____
_____	_____

Unusual Jobs / Activities for Women	**Reason I Think It's Unusual**
_____	_____
_____	_____
_____	_____

3. Now share your findings with the class.

Listening Task

Listen to your classmates' reports. Which job or activity do you think is the most unusual for a man? Which job or activity do you think is most unusual for a woman?

For Unit 6 Internet activities, visit the NorthStar Companion Website at http://www.longman.com/northstar.

Good-Mood Foods

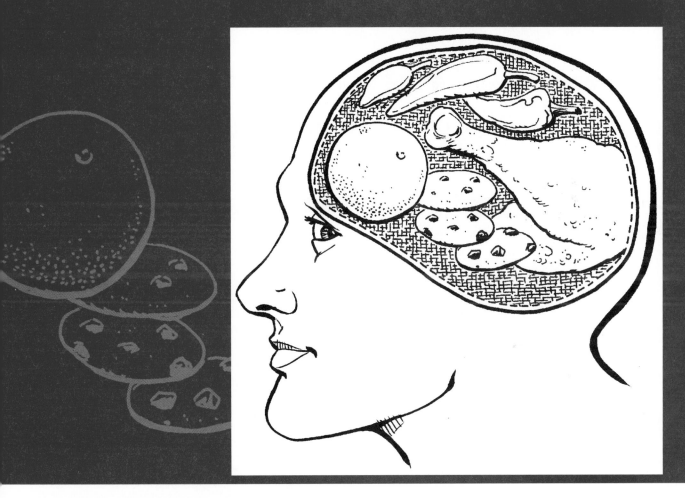

1 Focus on the Topic

A PREDICTING

Look at the picture, and discuss these questions with the class.

1. What does the picture show? Name the foods you see.

2. What do you think the picture means?

3. Read the title of the unit. What do you think it means?

B   SHARING INFORMATION

1 *Why do you choose a particular food? Number these reasons in order of importance from **1** to **5**. Number 1 is the most important to you and number 5 is the least important.*

_____ It tastes good.   _____ It's easy to cook.

_____ It's good for you.   _____ Everyone at my house likes it.

_____ It's cheap.

2 *Now work in a small group. Explain why your reason number 1 is the most important to you.*

Example: A: I want food that's cheap because I have a big family.

B: I want food that's easy to cook because I'm a bad cook.

C   PREPARING TO LISTEN

BACKGROUND

People have different reasons for choosing foods. You may choose a food because it's good for you. The food pyramid below is from the American Heart Association. It shows how many servings from each food group you need to stay healthy. People should eat more foods from the groups at the bottom of the pyramid, like fruits and vegetables. They are very good for you because they have a lot of vitamins and minerals. On the other hand, people should eat fewer servings of the foods from the groups at the top of the pyramid because they aren't as good for you.

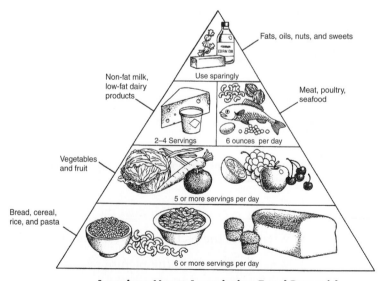

American Heart Association Food Pyramid

1 *Work in pairs. Look at the food groups in the pyramid. Answer the following questions.*

1. What are the names of the different food groups?

2. What food group does each of the following foods belong to?

chili peppers _____   turkey _____

chocolate   _____   wheat _____

oranges   _____

3. According to the food pyramid, what are some foods that are good for you? What are some foods that are not as good for you? Do you agree with the food pyramid? Why or why not?

2 *Look at the following foods. What are they made with? Name two ingredients in each one. Do you think either of these foods are good for you? Is either bad for you?*

1. Turkey Sandwich

Ingredients:

_____

_____

2. Chocolate Chip Cookies

Ingredients:

_____

_____

VOCABULARY FOR COMPREHENSION

1 *In the following conversations, the people are talking about their feelings or their moods (the way they feel at a particular time). Read each conversation. Then circle the correct definition of the underlined word(s).*

1. A: What are you thinking about?

   B: Oh, I'm thinking about my girlfriend. She's so great! I want to be with her all the time.

   A: Wow. It sounds like you're <u>in love</u>.

   a. feel love for someone   **b.** love to do something

2. A: What are you doing after work?

   B: First, I'm going to the gym to get some exercise. Then I'm going to go out dancing.

   A: Wow! You're feeling very <u>energetic</u> today!

   a. full of energy   **b.** without energy

3. A: What's the matter? You look <u>miserable</u>.

   B: I am. I just lost my job and I feel really bad about it.

   A: Oh, I'm sorry to hear that.

   a. very angry   **b.** extremely unhappy

4. A: Do you want to go to the movies with me?

B: No way! I don't have time to go to the movies!

A: Gee, you sure are <u>irritable</u> today.

B: Sorry. I'm having a bad day.

   a. easily angered or annoyed   **b.** busy and unable to have fun

5. A: You look <u>upbeat</u> today. What are you smiling about?

B: I'm going on vacation with my family today. I think it's going to be a lot of fun.

A: Good for you. Have a good time!

   a. happy or cheerful   **b.** funny

6. A: It's almost your turn to give a speech in front of the class. How do you feel?

B: I feel really <u>nervous</u>. I hate speaking in front of people. My knees are shaking!

   a. sad or unhappy   **b.** worried or afraid

7. A: You gave a great speech. You looked so <u>relaxed</u>. How do you stay so calm?

B: I'm lucky. I like speaking in front of people. I never get nervous.

   a. lucky   **b.** calm; not nervous

8. A: What's wrong? You look worried about something.

B: Yes, I feel really <u>stressed</u> right now. I have a lot of work to do, and my mother is sick.

A: I'm sorry to hear that.

   a. worried or pressured   **b.** in a hurry

2 *All the words in Exercise 1 describe feelings or moods. Some are good and some are bad. Make a list of good and bad feelings or moods on a separate piece of paper. Compare your list with a partner's.*

Example: *Good Feelings / Moods*   *Bad Feelings / Moods*

        1. feeling relaxed   *1. feeling irritable*

Now write a sentence that explains when you might be in each mood. Compare your list with a partner's.

Example: *Good Feelings / Moods*   *Bad Feelings / Moods*

        1. I feel relaxed after I take a nap.   *1. I feel irritable when I'm hungry.*

2 Focus on Listening

A   LISTENING ONE: *Would You Like to Be on the Radio?*

 Listen to these excerpts from a radio talk show. Read the questions and discuss the answers with the class.

1. Where are the people?

3. How do the people feel?

2. What are the people doing?

4. What will they talk about?

LISTENING FOR MAIN IDEAS

 *Now listen to the whole radio show called "Street Talk." Then read each statement and decide if it is true or false. Write **T** (true) or **F** (false) next to it.*

_____ 1. Some doctors think that foods can change your moods.

_____ 2. Some doctors say that eating certain foods will put you in a bad mood.

_____ 3. Marty wants to help the people feel better.

LISTENING FOR DETAILS

*Listen to "Street Talk" again. Look at the chart and answer the questions. **(1)** Check (✓) the correct mood for each person. **(2)** Check (✓) the foods that Marty tells each person to eat. **(3)** Check (✓) the moods for each food.*

	1. How does the person feel now?		2. What food(s) can help the person feel better?		3. How can the food(s) help the person feel?			
					Energetic	In Love	Relaxed	Upbeat
Larry	excited	❏	chili peppers	❏	❏	❏	❏	❏
	nervous	❏	chocolate	❏	❏	❏	❏	❏
Dan	miserable	❏	chocolate	❏	❏	❏	❏	❏
	stressed	❏	nuts	❏	❏	❏	❏	❏
			wheat flour	❏	❏	❏	❏	❏
Barbara	stressed	❏	turkey	❏	❏	❏	❏	❏
	nervous	❏	orange juice	❏	❏	❏	❏	❏
			bread	❏	❏	❏	❏	❏

Now go back to Section 2A (question 4) above. Were your predictions correct?

REACTING TO THE LISTENING

 1 *Listen to two excerpts from the radio talk show. After listening to each excerpt, read the first question and circle the correct answer. Then answer the following question. Discuss your answers with the class.*

Excerpt One

1. How does the man feel about tasting the soup?

   a. interested

   b. scared

   How do you know?

2. How does the man feel after he tastes the soup?

   a. angry

   b. surprised

   How do you know?

Excerpt Two

1. How does the woman feel when Marty offers her the food?

   a. scared

   b. angry

   How do you know?

2. How do you think she speaks to Marty?

   a. politely

   b. rudely

   Why do you think so?

2 *Discuss the following questions with the class. Give your opinions.*

1. Do you think foods can change your moods?

2. Do you ever eat foods to change your moods? If so, which foods do you eat?

3. What other things do you do to change your moods? For example, what do you usually do to feel relaxed, upbeat, or energetic?

B   LISTENING TWO: *What's the Matter?*

 Listen to four people: Kate, Derek, Jane, and Jeff. How does each one feel? Why do they feel that way? Write your answers in the chart on page 105.

	Kate	Derek	Jane	Jeff
1. How does the person feel?				
2. Why does he or she feel that way?				

C   LINKING LISTENINGS ONE AND TWO

Work with a partner. Decide what food(s) Kate, Derek, Jane, and Jeff should eat to feel better. You can choose foods from the box below or think of your own.

bread	oranges
chili peppers	turkey
chocolate	

	Food(s)
Kate	
Derek	
Jane	
Jeff	

Now, discuss your answers with the class. Why did you choose that food? What else do you think the person should do to feel better?

3 Focus on Vocabulary

1 *Work with a partner. Each of the words and phrases in the box can be used with one of the verbs in the chart. Some words and phrases can be used with more than one verb. Complete the chart. Then think of two more words or phrases to add to each column.*

alone	chili peppers	good for you	in a good mood	stupid
angry	crazy	hot	in a hurry	stressed
bad	delicious	in a bad mood	rude	turkey

Be	Feel	Look	Made with	Smell	Taste
hot	hot	hot			hot

2 *Discuss the words in Exercise 1 with your class. Take turns making sentences using the words and the verbs from the chart.*

Example: A: The soup is too hot to eat.

B: It feels hot in this room.

3 *Work in pairs. Take turns asking the questions below. Use at least two words from the box in each answer.*

Verbs	Adjectives		
be (is, are)	alone	hot	rude
feel	angry	in a bad mood	stressed
look	bad	in a good mood	stupid
made with	crazy	in a hurry	upbeat
smell	delicious	irritable	
taste	good / bad for you	miserable	

1. Are you in a good mood or a bad mood today? Why?

2. How often are you in a hurry to get to school or work?

3. When do you feel angry? What do you do when you feel angry?

4. Look at (*name of a classmate*). How does he or she look today?

5. What's your favorite food? What's it made with?

4 Focus on Speaking

A   PRONUNCIATION: Vowels: [ʊ] and [uw]

[ʊ] is the vowel sound in the word *good* /gʊd/.
[uw] is the vowel sound in the word *mood* /muwd/.

good [ʊ]   **mood [uw]**

When you say [ʊ], your lips are
rounded a little and your tongue
is relaxed.

When you say [uw], your lips are
tightly rounded and your tongue
is raised in the back.

[ʊ] is a short sound.

[uw] is a long sound.

 1 *Listen and repeat this sentence.*

I read a good book about mood foods.

 2 *Listen to the words. Do the underlined letters have the [ʊ] vowel sound or the [uw]
vowel sound? Write the words in the box under the correct vowel column. Compare
your answers with those of a classmate.*

1. s<u>oo</u>n	5. s<u>ou</u>p	9. w<u>ou</u>ld	13. j<u>ui</u>ce
2. l<u>oo</u>k	6. L<u>u</u>ke	10. c<u>oo</u>kies	14. b<u>oo</u>k
3. c<u>oo</u>l	7. t<u>oo</u>	11. n<u>ew</u>s	15. n<u>oo</u>n
4. c<u>oo</u>k	8. c<u>ou</u>ld	12. f<u>oo</u>d	16. fr<u>ui</u>t

good [ʊ]	**mood [uw]**
	soon

 3 *Listen again and repeat the words.*

4 Listen to each phrase or sentence. Are the underlined vowel sounds the same or different? Write **S** (same) in the blank if the vowel sounds are the same. Write **D** (different) if they are different.

_____ **1.** a good cook

_____ **2.** fruit juice

_____ **3.** good soup

_____ **4.** Look at Luke.

_____ **5.** It's too soon.

_____ **6.** good news

_____ **7.** Cook the fruit.

_____ **8.** Cool the soup.

5 Work in pairs. Student A, ask one of the questions. Student B, listen to the question, choose an answer, and read it aloud. Change roles after item 3.

Example: A: What would you like to drink?

B: I'd like some fruit juice, please.

Student A

1. What would you like to drink?

2. Should I look at Robert?

3. I got an A on my English test.

4. What should I do with the fruit?

5. What do you think about my soup?

6. What time do you want to meet?

Student B

a. Mmm, you're a good cook.

b. I'd like some fruit juice, please.

c. No, look at Luke.

d. That's good news.

e. I could do it at noon.

f. Cook the fruit first.

B   **STYLE: Politely Expressing Wants**

When ordering food in a restaurant, or when eating at home, it's polite to use *would like* and *will have* to express wants.

Asking about Wants	Expressing Wants
What **would** you **like?**	**I'd like** a turkey sandwich, please.
Would you **like** anything to drink?	**I'll have** a cup of coffee, please.
Would you **like** anything else?	Yes, please. **I'll have** a glass of water.
	Refusing
	No, thank you.
	No, that'll be all, thanks.
	Just the check, please.

1 *Put the conversation in the correct order. Number the lines from **1** to **6**.*

Waiter / Waitress

_____ Would you like anything to drink with that?

_____ Would you like anything else?

_____ Good evening, are you ready to order?

Customer

_____ No, that'll be all, thanks.

_____ Yes, I'd like a hamburger.

_____ Yes, please. I'll have some iced tea.

2 *Work in pairs. Do a role play. Student A, you are a customer in a restaurant. Look at the menu below. Order a meal. Student B, you are a waiter or waitress. Take your partner's order. Then change roles.*

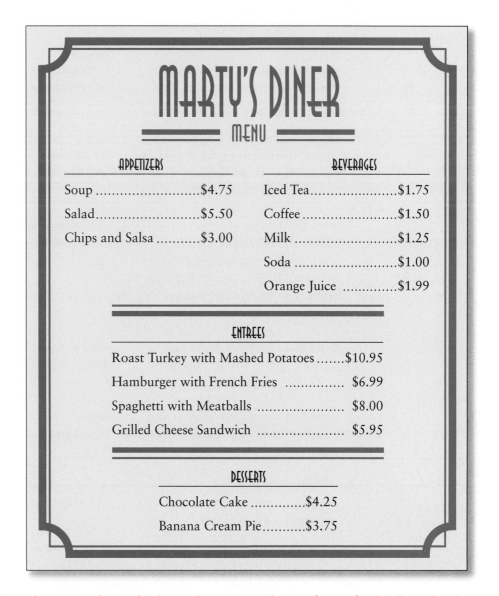

MARTY'S DINER
MENU

APPETIZERS

Soup $4.75

Salad $5.50

Chips and Salsa $3.00

BEVERAGES

Iced Tea $1.75

Coffee $1.50

Milk $1.25

Soda $1.00

Orange Juice $1.99

ENTREES

Roast Turkey with Mashed Potatoes $10.95

Hamburger with French Fries $6.99

Spaghetti with Meatballs $8.00

Grilled Cheese Sandwich $5.95

DESSERTS

Chocolate Cake $4.25

Banana Cream Pie $3.75

Now choose your best role play and practice it. Then perform it for the class. The class listens and writes down the customer's order.

C   GRAMMAR: Count and Non-count Nouns

1 *Read the sentences. Notice the underlined words. Then answer the questions.*

- We'll have two <u>hamburgers</u>.

- Would you like some <u>soup</u>, too?

a. Is the word *hamburgers* singular or plural? Can you count hamburgers?

b. Is the word *soup* singular or plural? Can you count soup? What word comes before *soup* in the sentence?

Count and Non-count Nouns*

		Singular	Plural
1. **Count nouns** refer to people or things that can be counted. They can be singular or plural.		one **customer** one **restaurant**	two **customers** two **restaurants**
	Use *a* or *an* before a singular count noun. To form the plural of a count noun, add **-s** or **-es.** You may use numbers with count nouns.	I ate **a** sandwich and **an** orange. He ate **two** sandwich**es, three** orange**s,** and **five** banana**s.**	
2. **Non-count nouns** refer to things that cannot be counted. Do not put *a*, *an*, or a number before a non-count noun. Do not add -s or -es to a non-count noun because non-count nouns do not have a plural form.		I like **orange juice.** We love **fish.**	
	Use a **quantity word** (*a glass of, a pound of,* etc.) to indicate the amount of a non-count noun.	Have **a glass of** orange juice. We need **a pound of** fish.	
3. Use *some* with plural count nouns and non-count nouns in affirmative statements.		I bought **some** apples. Have **some** milk.	
4. Use *any* with plural count nouns and non-count nouns in questions and negative statements.		A: Do we have **any** vegetables? B: No, we don't have **any** vegetables. A: Do we have **any** soup? B: No, we don't have **any** soup.	

---

* Count nouns and non-count nouns can also be called *countable nouns* and *uncountable nouns.*

2 *Work in pairs. Play a game of Tic-Tac-Toe.*

*Student A and Student B, take turns naming the foods in the squares. If the food is a singular count noun, say **a** or **an** before it. If the food is a plural count noun or non-count noun, say **some**. If you name a food correctly, put a marker on top of it. The first student to name three foods in a row correctly wins.*

3 Work in pairs. Take turns asking about the food on the shopping list. Use the question and answers in the box below.

Question	Answers
Do we need any . . . ?	Yes, we need . . .
	No, we don't need any . . .

Example: A: Do we need any rice?

B: Yes, we need some rice. Do we need any chili peppers?

A: No, we don't need any chili peppers.

Shopping List
rice

~~chili peppers~~

flour

bananas

milk

~~coffee~~

~~apples~~

bread

~~sugar~~

~~carrots~~

orange juice

~~soup~~

D   SPEAKING TOPICS

A potluck is a party where each guest brings a different dish to eat. Work in a small group to plan a potluck party. Follow these steps.

1. Each student chooses a different dish to bring to the party. Make sure your group has at least one appetizer, one main dish, and one dessert. Take turns asking and answering the questions below and write your answers in the chart.

    a. Would you like to bring an appetizer, a main dish, or a dessert?

    b. What dish would you like to bring?

    c. Why do you like it?

    d. What are the main ingredients?

	Dish	Why you like it	Main ingredients
Appetizer(s)			
Main Dish(es)			
Dessert(s)			

2. Each group reports to the class about the dishes they will bring.

Listening Task

The class listens to the reports and answers these questions.

1. Which dishes do you think will taste good?

2. Which dishes are good for you?

3. Which dishes are good for your moods?

E ■ RESEARCH TOPIC

You're going to research a restaurant. Work with another student or in a small group. Follow these steps.

1. Choose a restaurant where you would like to eat. Go to the restaurant for a meal. Then answer the following questions about the restaurant.

   a. What's the name of the restaurant?

   _____

   b. Where is it?

   _____

   c. What did you eat and drink?

   _____

   d. How did the food look, smell, and taste?

   _____

e. How did the restaurant look?

_____

f. Was the waiter or waitress polite?

_____

g. How did you feel after your meal?

_____

2. Report back to your class with a review of the restaurant. Would you recommend the restaurant to your classmates?

Listening Task

Listen to your classmates' reports. Which restaurant(s) do you want to go to? Why?
Which restaurant(s) don't you want to go to? Why not?

For Unit 7 Internet activities, visit the NorthStar Companion Website at http://www.longman.com/northstar.

An Ice Place to Stay

1 Focus on the Topic

A PREDICTING

Look at the photograph, and discuss these questions with the class.

1. Where do you think this picture was taken?

2. What is the man doing there?

3. What is the man wearing? What time of year do you think it is?

4. Read the title of the unit. What do you think it means?

B ■ SHARING INFORMATION

1 *This is a list of things people think about when choosing a place to visit. Some things are more important than others. Check (✓)* **Very Important, Somewhat Important,** *or* **Not Important.**

	Very Important	Somewhat Important	Not Important
weather (what the weather's like)	❏	❏	❏
location (how far it is from home)	❏	❏	❏
language (what language the people speak)	❏	❏	❏
cost (how expensive it is to visit)	❏	❏	❏
activities (things to do there)	❏	❏	❏
sights (places to see there)	❏	❏	❏
lodging (places to stay there)	❏	❏	❏
people (friends and family to visit)	❏	❏	❏

2 *Now compare your answers in a group. Tell why each item is very important, somewhat important, or not important to you.*

3 *Discuss this question with your group.*

Where can you get information to plan a vacation?

C ■ PREPARING TO LISTEN

BACKGROUND

Look at this map of northern Europe. Then read the information about Sweden on page 117.

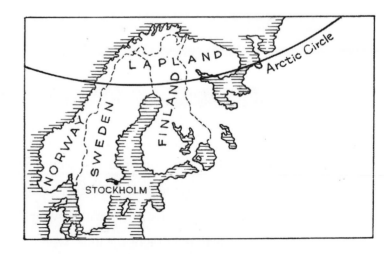

Sweden is a very large country in northern Europe. It covers 977 miles from north to south. Every year tourists come from all over the world to visit Sweden's cities, see the interesting sights, and enjoy the outdoors. It's easy to find nature in Sweden. Fifty percent of Sweden is covered with forests of beautiful trees, and many wild animals live there. There are 96,000 lakes in Sweden and in the north there is a long range of tall mountains.

Tourists planning a trip to Sweden must think about the weather when choosing the best time to visit. In summer, the days are long and warm. The sun shines almost all day and night, and in the north, visitors can see the midnight sun. Winter, on the other hand, is cold and dark. Sometimes there are only a few hours of sunlight each day.

Tourists must also think about costs when planning a trip to Sweden. Shops, restaurants, and lodging are all very expensive. So if you're on a budget, you'll need to watch your money in Sweden.

Now work in a small group. Discuss the following questions.

1. Where is Sweden?

2. What's the weather like in the summer? What's the weather like in the winter?

3. What time of year do you think tourists usually visit Sweden? Why do you think so?

4. What activities do you think you can do there in the summer? What activities do you think you can do there in the winter?

5. Have you ever visited Sweden? If not, would you like to visit Sweden? Why or why not?

VOCABULARY FOR COMPREHENSION

1 *Read these paragraphs. Notice the underlined words. If you don't know a word, look it up in the dictionary. Then discuss the meanings of the words with the class.*

Tourists planning a trip to Sweden have many different kinds of vacations to choose from. People who prefer big cities may choose to visit Stockholm, Sweden's largest city. In Stockholm, tourists can go shopping, visit <u>museums</u> to learn about the local history and culture, and go to <u>art galleries</u> to see some Swedish art. In and around Stockholm there are also some beautiful old <u>churches</u> and castles to visit. In the evening, tourists can eat out in restaurants and go to a concert or a show.

Tourists who enjoy nature can find many outdoor activities to do in Sweden. In the summer months, they can go swimming or hiking or just relax on the beach. Those who enjoy cold-weather activities, such as <u>skiing</u> and ice skating, can visit Sweden in the winter, when there is always a lot of snow and ice on the ground.

(continued)

There are also many different kinds of <u>lodging</u>, or places to stay, in Sweden. Travelers can stay at large <u>hotels</u> or they can choose to be <u>guests</u> at small country <u>inns</u>, where they may be treated to a home-cooked breakfast. Budget travelers may prefer to stay at a youth hostel, where they can share a room for very little money. Those who really want to save money and enjoy nature can stay at <u>campsites</u> and sleep outdoors under the trees in a <u>sleeping bag</u>.

2 *Look at the pictures. Look at the words below. Write the number of the picture next to the correct word.*

Picture 1

Picture 2

Picture 3

Picture 4

_____ cross-country skiing _____ snowmobiling

_____ dogsledding   _____ snowshoeing

3 *Read each group of four words. Cross out the word that does not belong. Then compare your answers with a partner. Explain why you think each word doesn't belong.*

1. church	art gallery	museum	lodging
2. inn	sleeping bag	hotel	campsite
3. dogsledding	snowshoeing	inn	cross-country skiing
4. guest	tourist	traveler	hotel

2 Focus on Listening

A   LISTENING ONE: *An Unusual Vacation*

 Listen to the beginning of "An Unusual Vacation." Read each question. Then circle the correct answer.

1. What are you listening to?
   a. a TV commercial
   b. a telephone recording
   c. a radio show

2. What is it about?
   a. travel information about Sweden
   b. airplane flights to Sweden
   c. winter activities in Sweden

3. What will you hear more about?
   a. campsites in Sweden
   b. large hotels in Sweden
   c. a special winter hotel in Sweden

4. Will you hear a conversation or a recording?
   a. a conversation
   b. a recording

5. What do you think it will tell you? (*Circle more than one answer.*)
   a. the name of the hotel
   b. the location of the hotel
   c. the cost of the hotel
   d. how to get to the hotel
   e. things to do at the hotel
   f. things to do near the hotel

LISTENING FOR MAIN IDEAS

 *Now listen to "An Unusual Vacation." Then read each statement and decide if it is true or false. Write **T** (true) or **F** (false) next to it.*

_____ 1. You can only go to the Ice Hotel in the summer.

_____ 2. The Ice Hotel is made of ice and snow.

_____ 3. The Ice Hotel is just like most hotels.

_____ 4. The rooms are warm at night.

_____ 5. There are only guest rooms at the Ice Hotel.

_____ 6. There are many activities to do near the Ice Hotel.

LISTENING FOR DETAILS

 Listen to "An Unusual Vacation" again. Check (✓) all the things you can find in the Ice Hotel and the things you can see or do near the Ice Hotel.

Things in the Ice Hotel
(Check five items.)

_____ **1.** guest rooms

_____ **2.** an art gallery

_____ **3.** a church

_____ **4.** beds

_____ **5.** doors

_____ **6.** bathrooms

_____ **7.** sleeping bags

Things near the Ice Hotel
(Check four items.)

_____ **1.** a movie theater

_____ **2.** cross-country skiing

_____ **3.** snowshoeing

_____ **4.** dogsledding

_____ **5.** snowmobiling

_____ **6.** ice skating

_____ **7.** a new church

Now go back to Section 2A (questions 3, 4, 5) on page 119. Were your predictions correct?

REACTING TO THE LISTENING

 1 *Listen to two excerpts from "An Unusual Vacation." After listening to each excerpt, answer the first question. Then read the other two questions and circle the correct answer for each. Discuss your answers with the class.*

Excerpt One

1. What is the Ice Hotel made of?

2. What does the man think of it?
   a. He thinks it sounds like a typical hotel.
   b. He is unsure.

3. How do you know?
   a. His voice rises.
   b. His voice falls.

Excerpt Two

1. How many hours of sunlight are there?

2. What does the man think of that?
   a. He's unsure.
   b. He thinks it's good.

3. How do you know?
   a. He speaks louder.
   b. He asks a question.

2 *Discuss these questions with another student, and then with the class. Give your opinions.*

1. The Ice Hotel costs over $150 a night. How much money is that in your country?

2. Do you think it's worth the price? Why or why not?

3. Imagine you are planning a vacation to Sweden. Will you go to the Ice Hotel? Why or why not?

B   LISTENING TWO: *Vacations around the World*

One way to get information to plan a vacation is to read travel brochures. You can get travel brochures about many different places from a travel agency.

1 *Look at the three travel brochures. What place does each brochure describe? What do you know about these places?*

Brochure A

HIMALAYAN
MOUNTAIN ADVENTURE
Do you love nature and beautiful scenery? Do you enjoy hiking and camping? Then this is the trip for you!

Activities:
Go _____
Enjoy _____
Meet _____
Lodging: _____
Time of Year: _____

Brochure B

SOUTHERN CALIFORNIA VACATION
This travel package will take you to Hollywood and Disneyland, the happiest places on Earth!

Activities:
Visit _____
Take a tour of _____
Go _____
Visit _____
Lodging: _____
Time of Year: _____

Brochure C

BALINESE
CULTURAL HOLIDAY
Travel to the Indonesian island of Bali for a relaxing and educational vacation.

Activities:
Relax _____
Study _____
Learn how to _____
Lodging: _____
Time of Year: _____

_____   _____   _____

 2 *Listen to "Vacations around the World." It gives information about three different vacations. These vacations are in the places described by the brochures. Write the number of the vacation under the correct brochure.*

 3 *Listen again to "Vacations around the World." Then complete the brochures. Write the activities, lodging, and time of year to travel for each vacation.*

C   LINKING LISTENINGS ONE AND TWO

*You have heard about four different places where you could go on a vacation. Read the following questions and write **A**, **B**, **C**, or **D** next to each one. Then compare your answers in a group. Explain your answers.*

A = The Himalayan Mountains	**C** = Bali, Indonesia
B = Southern California	**D** = The Ice Hotel, Sweden

_____ **1.** Which place do you think is best for weather?

_____ **2.** Which place do you think is best for lodging?

_____ **3.** Which place do you think is best for indoor activities?

_____ **4.** Which place do you think is best for outdoor activities?

_____ **5.** Which place do you think is best for sights to see?

_____ **6.** Which place would you like to visit?

3 Focus on Vocabulary

1 *Read the sentences. Then match the underlined phrases with the definitions on the right.*

__*g*__ **1.** If you <u>are adventurous</u>, I think you would like the Ice Hotel.

_____ **2.** In the winter, I like to <u>go cross-country skiing</u>.

_____ **3.** The mountains are a great place to <u>go hiking</u>.

_____ **4.** Children love to <u>go to amusement parks</u>.

_____ **5.** Weekends are a time to <u>have fun</u>.

_____ **6.** When I travel, I like to <u>look at the scenery</u> of the new places I go.

_____ **7.** On warm days, it's nice to <u>relax on the beach</u> near the ocean.

_____ **8.** Travelers without a lot of money often like to <u>stay at youth hostels</u>.

_____ **9.** In a new city, it's often good to <u>take a tour</u> of all the sights.

a. enjoy yourself

b. go to parks where you can go on rides, play games, and see shows

c. lie on the beach and rest

d. look at the outdoor surroundings or views

e. stay at inexpensive lodging, usually for young travelers

f. visit a place or places, usually with a tour guide

g. like to try new and unusual things

h. go skiing over the countryside

i. take long walks outdoors, usually in nature

2 *Now use some of the phrases from Exercise 1 to complete the chart below. Then compare your answers with the class. Think of two more activities to add to each list.*

Indoor activities	Outdoor activities	Indoor or outdoor activities

3 *Work in pairs. Take turns saying whether you like or don't like to do the activities from Exercise 2. Explain your answers.*

4 *Work in a small group. Take turns responding to the statements. Each student in the group speaks. Use the underlined words in your answers.*

1. Describe a time you were a <u>guest</u> somewhere.

2. Describe an <u>adventurous</u> person.

3. Describe your favorite kind of <u>scenery</u>.

4. Describe your favorite kind of <u>lodging</u>.

5. Describe a <u>tour</u> you have taken or want to take some day.

6. Describe your favorite way to <u>have fun</u>.

7. Describe your favorite way to <u>relax</u>.

4 Focus on Speaking

A   PRONUNCIATION: *Can* and *Can't*

Can: In affirmative statements and questions, we don't stress *can*. It is pronounced /kən/ and sounds like the last syllable of *bacon* or *Mexican*. The vowel in *can* is short and unclear.

Can't: Stress the negative word *can't*. The vowel in *can't* is clear and long /kænt/.

Note that *can* in short answers is stressed. The vowel is clear and long /kæn/.

Listen to these examples:

You can only go to the Ice Hotel in winter.
You can't go in summer.

A: Can I go snowshoeing near the hotel?
B: Yes, you can.

1 *Listen and repeat the phrases and sentences. Pronounce* **can** *as* /kən/. *Join* **can** *to the preceding word.*

  1. Mr. Bay can—bacon: Mr. Bay can cook bacon.

  2. Joe can—chicken: Joe can cook chicken.

  3. Maxy can—Mexican: Maxy can cook Mexican food.

2 *Listen to the dialogue and repeat the lines.*

TRAVEL AGENT: You can ski near the Ice Hotel.

CUSTOMER: Can you shop?

TRAVEL AGENT: No, you can't shop.

3 *Listen to these sentences. Are they affirmative (***can***) or negative (***can't***)? Check (✓) the correct column for each sentence.*

Affirmative	Negative	Affirmative	Negative
1.		**4.**	
2.		**5.**	
3.		**6.**	

4 *Listen again. Write the sentences on the lines. Then say them to a partner.*

1. _____

2. _____

3. _____

4. _____

5. _____

6. _____

5 *Work in pairs. Take turns reading the sentences from Exercise 4. Stress **can't** by saying it louder or longer. Do not stress **can**. Explain why each sentence is true or false according to what you heard in Listening One.*

B   STYLE: Making Polite Requests

When you want to make a polite request or to politely ask for something, use *can, could,* or *would*. Note that *could* and *would* are more polite than *can*. To make your request even more polite, use *please* in addition.

Requesting Politely	Answering Politely
Excuse me. **Can** you **please** tell me where the restroom is?	**Certainly.** It's on the first floor.
Could you tell me the hours of the post office, **please?**	**Sure, it's** open from 8:00 to 5:00.
Would you **please** tell me the cost of an airplane ticket to New York?	**Sorry, I don't know.**
Thanking	**Replying to Thanks**
Thank you.	**Don't mention it.**
Thanks a lot.	**No problem.**
Well, thanks anyway.*	**You're welcome.**

* Used only when the information requested is not available or not useful.

Work in pairs. Student A, look at this page. Student B, look at Student Activities, page 164. Follow the instructions there.

Student A, you are a clerk at the information desk of the Himalaya Inn in Katmandu, Nepal. Look at your list of information and answer your partner's requests.

THE HIMALAYA INN
KATMANDU, NEPAL

TOURIST INFORMATION

Local Restaurants
The Hungry Eye
Kind of food: Indian
Location: across the street
Cost of a meal: about $2

Fuji Restaurant
Kind of food: Japanese
Location: Near the Royal Palace
Cost of a meal: about $8

Post Office
Hours: Sunday–Friday, 8 A.M. to 7 P.M.
Saturday, 11 A.M. to 3 P.M.

Bank
Hours: Sunday–Thursday, 10 A.M. to 2 P.M.
Friday, 10 A.M. to noon

The Royal Palace
Hours: 10:30 A.M. to 4 P.M. daily
Cost to enter: about 20 cents

Now change roles. Student A, you are a guest staying at the Sunset Hotel in Los Angeles, California. Ask Student B polite questions to get the following information. Write the answers. If you don't know how to spell a word, ask Student B to spell it for you.

1. The location of the Hard Rock Cafe: _____
2. The cost of a meal at The Dining Room restaurant: _____
3. The telephone number of the tourist office: _____
4. The hours of Disneyland on Friday: _____
5. The cost of a ticket to Disneyland for children: _____
6. The hours of Universal Movie Studios: _____

C   GRAMMAR: *Can* and *Can't*

1 *Read the sentences. Notice the underlined words. Then answer the questions below.*

- What <u>can</u> you <u>do</u> at the Ice Hotel?
- You <u>can look</u> at paintings in the art gallery.
- You <u>can't go</u> swimming.

a. What are the verbs in each sentence? In what form is the main verb?

b. What does *can* mean? What does *can't* mean?

Can and *Can't*

Can is a modal. Modals are words that come before verbs. They change the meanings of the verbs in some way.

1. Use *can* to talk about ability, things you are able to do.	I **can** ice skate. I took lessons last year.
Use *can't* to talk about inability.	My brother **can't** ski. He's never tried it.
2. Use *can* to talk about possibility, things that are possible.	You **can** stay at the Ice Hotel in the winter when the weather is cold.
Use *can't* to talk about things that are not possible.	You **can't** stay at the Ice Hotel in the summer because it isn't there.

		BASE FORM	
You	**can**	**go**	ice skating in Sweden.
I	**can't**	**go**	on vacation right now.

3. *Can* and *can't* come before the main verb. The main verb is in the **base form.**	
4. Use *can* and *can't* in questions and short answers. Do not use a main verb in a short answer.	A: **Can** you swim? B: Yes, I **can.**
	A: **Can** Ellen ice skate? B: No, she **can't.**

2 *Work in a group of three students. You want to find out your partners' abilities. Before you interview them, write their names in the chart on page 128. Write also five yes/no questions to ask them. Then interview your partners and note their answers in the chart.*

Example: A: Can you dance?

B: Yes, I can.

C: No, I can't.

Yes/no questions	name	name
1. Can you dance?	Yes	No
2.		
3.		
4.		
5.		

Now report to the class. Pay attention to your pronunciation of **can** *and* **can't.**

Example: Miguel can dance, but Hiroshi can't. OR

Miguel can dance, and Hiroshi can dance, too.

3 *Work in pairs. Look at the ad for Quebec's Ice Hotel. Take turns making statements about what is possible to do at or near Quebec's Ice Hotel. Your partner will agree or disagree with you. Pay attention to your pronunciation of* **can** *and* **can't.**

Example: A: You can see ice sculptures at Quebec's Ice Hotel.

B: That's right. You can.

B: You can swim at Quebec's Ice Hotel.

A: No, you can't. There isn't a pool.

Come to Quebec's Ice Hotel!
Near Quebec City, Quebec, Canada

❄ Have your wedding, reunion, or birthday

❄ See ice sculptures of Canada's Great North
Watch a movie in the theater
Sit on ice furniture
Sleep on an ice bed

❄ Go cross-country skiing
Go snowmobiling

❄ Visit nearby Montgomery Falls Park
See the 83-meter (272-feet) waterfall
Dine at a fine restaurant

D SPEAKING TOPICS

You are going to do a role play with a partner. One student will be a tourist. The other student will be a travel agent. Follow these steps.

1. Choose a vacation place to talk about. It can be a city or a country you lived in or visited. Fill in information about your place in the chart below. Write its name and then write about the weather, best time of year to visit, activities, sights to see, and lodging.

2. Now find out the name of your partner's place and write it in the chart. Then write the questions in the chart that you will ask about that place during the role play. Use *can, could*, and *would* in your questions. See the example.

Topics	Your place _____ name	Questions	Your partner's place _____ name
Weather		*Could you tell me about the weather in _____ ?*	
Best time of year to visit			
Activities			
Sights to see			
Lodging			

3. Now do the role play with your partner. Student A, you are the tourist. You want to travel to your partner's place. Ask the travel agent (Student B) the questions in your chart. Student B, you are the travel agent. Answer the tourist's (Student A's) questions.

   Example

   A: Could you please give me some information about _____ ?

   B: Sure. What would you like to know?

   A: Could you tell me about the weather in _____ ?

4. When you are finished, change roles.

5. Practice your best conversation for the class.

Listening Task

Listen to your classmates' role plays and fill out the card below.

Which place would you like to visit?
Name of the place:
Two activities you can do there:
Two sights you can see there:

E   RESEARCH TOPIC

You're going to research a place you would like to visit. Work in pairs. Follow these steps.

1. Think of a country or a city that you would both like to visit. Write a list of questions to get information about the topics listed in the card below.

2. Go to a travel agency or call the travel bureau for the country. One of you asks the questions. The other one fills out the card. If you can, get some travel brochures about the place.

Country or City:
Weather:
Best time of year to visit:
Activities:
Sights to see:
Lodging:
Cost:

3. Tell the class about the place you want to visit. Show them any brochures or pictures you have.

Listening Task

Listen to your classmates' presentations. Which place sounds most interesting? Why?

For Unit 8 Internet activities, visit the NorthStar Companion Website at http://www.longman.com/northstar.

Staying Healthy

1 Focus on the Topic

A PREDICTING

Look at the cartoon, and discuss these questions with the class.

1. What is the man doing in each picture? How does he feel?

2. Do you think the man is healthy or unhealthy? Why?

3. Read the title of the unit. What do you think the unit will be about?

B   SHARING INFORMATION

1 *Work in a small group. Make a list of activities that are good for your health and a list of activities that are bad for your health.*

Healthy Activities	**Unhealthy Activities**
walking	*smoking*
_____	_____
_____	_____
_____	_____

2 *Look at the lists you made in Exercise 1. Discuss these questions in your group.*

   1. Which of these activities do you do? How often?

   2. Which activity do you think is the best for your health? Why?

   3. Which activity is the worst for your health? Why?

C   PREPARING TO LISTEN

BACKGROUND

Read the following facts about weight and health in the United States.

Weight and Health

- More than 50 percent of Americans are overweight; they are too heavy.

- Overweight people have more health problems; they have more heart disease, high blood pressure, diabetes, and some kinds of cancer.

- Americans spend over $33 billion on weight-loss products every year.

- Americans try to lose weight in these ways:
    Exercising
    Going on a diet (eating less and/or eating certain foods)
    Using weight-loss remedies (using pills, powders, and drinks that help you to lose weight)
    Having weight-loss surgery (have an operation to help you lose weight)

- About 95 percent of people who lose weight will gain the weight back in one to five years.

- According to the U.S. National Institutes of Health, the best way to lose weight and keep it off is to eat less, exercise more, and lose weight slowly.

Now discuss these questions with a partner.

1. How many Americans are overweight? Why do you think so many people are overweight?

2. How much money do Americans spend to lose weight? What do you think they spend it on?

3. Why do you think so many people gain weight back after losing it?

4. What do the National Institutes of Health say is the best way to lose weight?

VOCABULARY FOR COMPREHENSION

Read the sentences and guess the meanings of the underlined words.

1. I saw a picture of a man who weighs 400 pounds. It's <u>amazing</u> that a person can be that heavy.

2. When I go on a diet I count all the <u>calories</u> I eat. I eat a lot of carrots because they only have a few calories, and I never eat cake or cookies because they have a lot of calories.

3. One way to lose weight is to stop eating <u>fattening foods</u> such as cheese, chocolate, or ice cream.

4. I have a really bad cold. I feel <u>terrible</u>.

5. I grow <u>herbs</u> such as parsley, cilantro, and mint in my garden. I use them for cooking and for making tea.

6. This medicine stopped my headache, but it gave me a stomachache. The stomachache was a surprising <u>side effect</u>.

7. I like <u>natural</u> fruit juice because it's made with real fruit, not artificial ingredients.

8. I need to lose some weight, so my doctor suggested I start exercising and <u>go on a diet</u>.

9. I was feeling unhealthy, but then I lost some weight and stopped smoking. Now I feel <u>terrific</u>!

10. I think aspirin is the best <u>remedy</u> for a headache. It always makes my headache go away.

11. One way to <u>prevent</u> health problems is to eat healthy foods, exercise every day, and get enough sleep. Doing those things will help to stop you from getting sick.

Now match the words with their definitions.

___d___ **1.** amazing   **a.** very good

_____ **2.** calories   **b.** very bad

_____ **3.** fattening foods   **c.** stop something from happening

_____ **4.** terrible   **d.** surprising; unbelievable

_____ **5.** herbs   **e.** foods that can make you fat

_____ **6.** side effect   **f.** eat less and/or eat certain foods to
                                       lose weight

_____ **7.** natural
                                   g. a measure of the energy in food that
_____ **8.** go on a diet   the body uses

_____ **9.** terrific
                                   h. an unexpected result that a medicine
_____ **10.** remedy   has on your body

_____ **11.** prevent
                                   i. coming from nature; not man-made
                                       or artificial

                                   j. plants used to make medicines or to
                                       flavor foods

                                   k. something you can do or take to
                                       correct a health problem

2 Focus on Listening

A   LISTENING ONE: *Thin-Fast*

 *Listen to a man talking about how to order Thin-Fast. Then read each question and
circle the correct answer.*

1. What are you listening to?
  a. a radio commercial   **b.** a radio news show   **c.** a conversation in a
                                                                    doctor's office

2. What is Thin-Fast?
  a. a diet book   **b.** a weight-loss remedy   **c.** an exercise machine

3. What do you think the listening will be about? (*Circle more than one answer.*)
  a. how to use Thin-Fast   **d.** what it's made of
  b. how old it is   **e.** how it makes you feel
  c. where it comes from   **f.** how much it costs

LISTENING FOR MAIN IDEAS

Listen to the whole radio commercial for Thin-Fast. Circle the correct answer to complete each statement.

1. Thin-Fast is a weight loss _____.
   a. pill
   b. drink
   c. powder

2. Mary Ann feels _____.
   a. overweight and unhappy
   b. thin and unhappy
   c. thin and happy

3. When using Thin-Fast, you _____.
   a. have to go on a diet
   b. have to exercise
   c. can eat fattening foods

4. The ingredients in Thin-Fast are _____.
   a. artificial
   b. natural

5. Mary Ann thinks that Thin-Fast tastes _____.
   a. great
   b. terrible

LISTENING FOR DETAILS

*Listen to the radio commercial again. Then read each statement and decide if it is true or false. Write **T** (true) or **F** (false) next to it. Then discuss your answers with the class.*

_____ 1. Mary Ann lost 75 pounds.

_____ 2. You drink Thin-Fast once a day.

_____ 3. Thin-Fast stops you from feeling hungry.

_____ 4. Thin-Fast prevents your body from taking in calories.

_____ 5. Thin-Fast has some side effects.

_____ 6. The ingredients in Thin-Fast have been used for 2,000 years.

_____ 7. Thin-Fast makes you feel energetic.

_____ 8. Thin-Fast comes in two different flavors.

_____ 9. You can buy Thin-Fast over the telephone.

Now go back to Section 2A (question 3) on page 134. Were your predictions correct?

REACTING TO THE LISTENING

1 *Read the information about commercials.*

> The purpose of commercials is to persuade the listeners (to get them to want to buy the product). Below are some strategies used in commercials to help persuade people.

Now listen to four excerpts from the Thin-Fast commercial. After listening to each excerpt, write the letter of the strategy you heard. You may hear more than one strategy in each excerpt.

Excerpts	Strategies Used in Commercials
1. _____	**a.** speaking with an excited tone of voice
2. _____	**b.** using strong words and statements
3. _____	**c.** using numbers
4. _____	**d.** asking questions using "you"
	e. asking a customer to talk about the product

2 *Read the information about opinions and facts.*

> Statements can be opinions or facts. An opinion is a statement that someone believes to be true. You can agree or disagree with an opinion. A fact is a statement that is true for everyone.

Now read each statement about Thin-Fast. Decide if it is an opinion or a fact. Check (✓) **Opinion** *or* **Fact.** *Then compare your answers with a partner's. Do you agree? Why or why not?*

	Opinion	Fact
1. Mary Ann lost 65 pounds in three months.	❏	❏
2. You drink one cup of Thin-Fast twice a day.	❏	❏
3. Thin-Fast is amazing.	❏	❏
4. Thin-Fast is a safe and healthy way to lose weight.	❏	❏
5. Thin-Fast tastes terrific.	❏	❏
6. Eight weeks of Thin-Fast costs $39.99.	❏	❏

3 *Would you use Thin-Fast? Why or why not? Discuss your answers with the class.*

4 *Mary Ann says she looks thin and feels healthy after losing weight. Why do you think most people want to lose weight, for their looks or for their health?*

B LISTENING TWO: *Health Problems and Remedies*

 Look at these pictures of two natural remedies. Then listen to two conversations and answer the questions in the chart below. Compare your answers with a partner's.

Peppermint

Garlic

	Conversation One	**Conversation Two**
1. Who is sick? What is the problem?		
2. What is the remedy suggested by the other person?		
3. Does the sick person want to try it?		

C LINKING LISTENINGS ONE AND TWO

*The chart below lists the health problems and remedies from Listening One and Listening Two. Answer the questions in the chart with **Yes, No,** or **Not sure**. Then work in a group. Discuss the different remedies. What is similar and what is different among them? Which remedies do you think are best? Why?*

	Overweight / *Thin-Fast Diet Tea*	**Stomachache / *peppermint tea***	**Cold / *garlic pills***
1. Is the remedy natural?			
2. Is it safe? Are there side effects?			
3. Is it inexpensive?			
4. Do you think it works?			

3 Focus on Vocabulary

1 *Complete the conversations with words or phrases from the box. Use the underlined words to help you. Then work in pairs. Practice reading the conversations out loud. Change roles after item 4.*

amazing	product	take care of yourself
herbal	remedy	terrible
prevent	side effects	terrific

1. A: I have a <u>very bad</u> headache.

   B: I'm sorry you have a such a _____ headache.

2. A: I make my own tea with <u>herbs</u> from my garden.

   B: Really? How do you make _____ tea?

3. A: I have a book that tells you <u>what to do or take for health problems</u>.

   B: Do you know a good _____ for a stomachache?

4. A: I just tried a new medicine that can <u>stop</u> you from getting a cold.

   B: I don't believe it. Can it really _____ colds?

Now change roles.

5. A: I want to <u>buy something to help me lose weight</u>.

   B: I don't think you should spend money on a weight-loss _____.

6. A: I <u>do a lot of healthy things:</u> I eat healthy food, I exercise, and I don't smoke.

   B: Wow! You really _____.

7. A: I really like my new doctor. He's <u>very good</u>.

   B: He sounds like a _____ doctor.

8. A: I just heard about a drug that can help you lose weight, but <u>it can also make you sick</u>.

   B: Yeah. Weight-loss drugs can often have bad _____.

9. A: My friend was very sick and the doctors thought he was going to die. Then he got better. <u>I couldn't believe it</u>.

   B: That's _____.

2 *Work in a small group. Take turns asking the questions. Each student in the group answers the questions. Use the underlined words in your answers.*

1. What do you think is the most important thing you can do to <u>prevent</u> health problems?

2. What do you do to <u>take care of</u> yourself?

3. Do you use any <u>herbal remedies</u>? If so, what do you use? Are there any <u>side effects</u>?

4. Do you think <u>natural</u> remedies are better than <u>artificial</u> remedies? Why or why not?

5. Have you ever seen or heard something <u>amazing</u>? If so, what did you see? Why was it amazing?

6. When do you feel <u>terrible</u>? What do you do to feel better?

7. When do you feel <u>terrific</u>?

4 Focus on Speaking

A   PRONUNCIATION: Rhythm—Content Words and Highlighting

Content and Function Words

When we speak, we stress some words and not others to make our meaning clear. Stressed words are usually content words (nouns, verbs, adjectives, and adverbs). Unstressed words are usually short function or grammar words (prepositions, pronouns, articles, and connecting words).

 Listen to these examples:

I was <u>overweight</u> and <u>unhealthy</u>.

Highlighting

In most sentences, one or two content words are the most important. We use our voice to highlight these words. Highlighted words are longer, louder, and higher-pitched than the other words.

• We usually highlight new important information.

 Listen to these examples:

I wanted to <u>lose weight</u>. So, I decided to try <u>thin-fast</u>.
Thin-Fast is a <u>safe</u> and <u>healthy</u> way to lose weight.

- We highlight strong words, such as *love, hate, really, always,* and *never.*

Listen to this example:

> I <u>loved</u> to eat fattening foods, and I <u>hated</u> to exercise.

- We also highlight words that show contrast.

Listen to these examples:

> Some weight-loss products are made with <u>artificial</u> ingredients, but Thin-Fast is made with only <u>natural</u> ingredients.

- In positive sentences, we often highlight the main verb. In negative sentences, we highlight the negatives.

Listen to these examples:

> I <u>looked</u> terrible, and I <u>felt</u> terrible.
> I just <u>couldn't</u> lose weight.

1 *Read the following sentences aloud. Underline the words you highlight. Compare your sentences with those of a partner. You and your partner may underline different words if you feel different words are important.*

1. Thin-Fast is amazing! It really works!

2. It's made from 100 percent natural herbs.

3. You just drink one cup of Thin-Fast twice a day.

4. You don't have to exercise, and you don't have to go on a diet.

5. You can eat fattening foods every day, and you'll never gain weight.

6. I lost 65 pounds in only three months.

7. Now I'm thin and happy.

2 *Now listen to the sentences and check your answers. Which words does the speaker highlight? Why do you think those words are highlighted?*

3 *Read the conversations and underline the highlighted words.*

1. A: What kind of tea are you drinking?

   B: Thin-Fast tea.

2. A: Should I drink it three times a day?

   B: No, you should only drink it twice a day.

3. A: Which flavor do you prefer?

   B: I like the orange flavor.

   A: Really? I prefer the lemon flavor.

4. A: Garlic is really good for your health.

   B: Really? But garlic is so bad for your breath.

   A: Not if you take garlic pills.

5. A: These chili peppers are delicious. I love chili peppers.

   B: I like them too, but I can't eat them.

   A: Really? That's too bad. You could try drinking peppermint tea. It's very
   good for stomachaches.

 4 *Now listen to the conversations and check your answers. Then practice saying the conversations with a partner.*

B STYLE: **Expressing Concern, Giving and Receiving Advice**

When someone has a problem, it's polite to express concern and offer some advice.

Expressing Concern

What's the matter?

What's wrong?

That's too bad.

I'm sorry to hear that.

Giving Advice

Maybe you should ...	go to the doctor.
Why don't you ...	try some peppermint tea?
I think you ought to ...	get some rest.
Have you tried ...	eating garlic?

Receiving Advice

That's a good idea.

Thanks for the advice. I'll give it a try.

Thanks anyway, but I'd rather ...

1 *Work in pairs. Look at the pictures and make up conversations. One student has a health problem. The other student expresses concern and gives some advice. Take turns. You can choose your advice from the box or make up your own.*

Example: A: What's the matter?

B: My wrist hurts. I've been typing too much.

A: That's too bad. Why don't you try acupuncture? It really works for pain.

B: Thanks. That's a good idea. I'll ask my doctor about it.

Wrist hurts.

go to the doctor	go home and rest	join a health club
get some medicine	eat healthier foods	try deep-breathing exercises
get more exercise	get a massage	try . . . (*remedy* or *treatment*)

1. Can't sleep.

2. Can't stop smoking.

3. Stressed out.

4. Out of shape.

2 *Now practice all the conversations. Then choose the best one and practice it for the class.*

C GRAMMAR: *Should, Ought to, Have to*

1 *Read the sentences. Notice the underlined words. Then answer the questions below.*

- You <u>should</u> try Thin-Fast Diet Tea.
- You <u>shouldn't</u> work so hard.
- You <u>ought to</u> take better care of yourself.
- You <u>have to</u> go to a doctor to have surgery.
- With Thin-Fast, you <u>don't have to</u> go on a diet.

a. What are the verbs in each sentence?

b. In what form is the main verb in each sentence?

c. What does *should* mean? What does *shouldn't* mean?

d. What does *ought to* mean?

e. What does *have to* mean? What does *don't have to* mean?

Should, Ought to, Have to

1. *Should, ought to,* and ***have to*** are modal verbs.

Use ***should*** and ***ought to*** to give advice or to talk about what is right to do.	If you're sick, you **should** see a doctor. She isn't well. You **ought to** call her.
Use ***shouldn't*** to talk about something that is not right to do.	You know you **shouldn't** drink. It's bad for you.
Use ***have to*** or ***has to*** to talk about something that you must do, something that is necessary.	I **have to** go to the drugstore. I need some medicine. He **has to** go to the hospital. He broke his arm.
Use ***don't have to*** or ***doesn't have to*** to talk about something that is not necessary.	You **don't have to** exercise if you drink Thin-Fast. She **doesn't have to** stay on a diet. She's thin now.

(continued)

2. In affirmative and negative **statements, *should, shouldn't,*** and ***ought to*** are followed by the base form of the verb. The modal verb and the main verb stay the same for each person.

		BASE FORM	
You	**should**	**exercise.**	
She	**ought to**	**lose**	weight.
We	**shouldn't**	**work**	so hard.

3. In **questions,** use ***should*** to ask for advice. ***Ought to*** is rarely used in questions or negatives.

Should I lose weight?
Why **should** he see the doctor?

4. Use ***have to*** and ***don't have to*** with *I, you, we,* and *they.*

I **have to** see the doctor.
You **don't have to** go to work when you're sick.

Use ***has to*** and ***doesn't have to*** with *he, she,* or *it.*

She **has to** take her medicine every day.
He **doesn't have to** have surgery.

2 *Complete the conversation with the correct modal verbs. Then practice the conversation with a partner.*

A: Hi. How are you?

B: Oh, not great. I'm so tired. I was up all night studying, and now I have soccer practice.

A: Oh, that's too bad. Maybe you **(1)** _____ go to practice today.

B: That's a good idea, but I have no choice. I **(2)** _____ to go because we have a big game tomorrow.

A: I know! You **(3)** _____ to try one of those energy drinks. I hear they can really pick you up when you're tired.

B: Really? (4) _____ I

really have an energy drink before

I exercise?

A: Why not? Energy drinks are full

of natural ingredients and vitamins.

And I heard that they can help

you play better at sports. A lot of

athletes use them these days. And the great thing is you

(5) _____ go to the doctor. You can just buy them at the market.

B: Well, I heard a news report about those energy drinks. It said that many

of them are unhealthy. They have a lot of caffeine and sugar, and you really

(6) _____ drink them before you exercise.

A: Wow, I didn't know that. Then I think you (7) _____ try the

most natural remedy.

B: Really? What's that?

A: Sleep!

D | SPEAKING TOPICS

You are going to write and perform a radio commercial with a partner. Follow these steps.

1. Write a radio commercial about an "amazing" health product. Use the
following situation. Choose a product from the list or think of your own.
Include the following information. Remember to use the modal verbs
should, ought to, and *have to* and phrases for giving advice.

Situation

One person has a health problem. The other person gives advice. The
"amazing" product solves the health problem.

Products	**Information**
Weight-loss product	Name of the product
Energy pills or drink	What it does
Product to help you stop smoking	How it works
Pain medicine	How often it should be used
Exercise machine	How much it costs
Sleep remedy	What it's made of (i.e., herbs)

2. Practice the commercial with your partner. Then present it to the class. If possible, tape record your commercial and give it to your teacher for feedback.

Listening Task

Listen to your classmates' commercials. For each product, write down the name of the health problem and the remedy. Discuss each product with the class. Would you use it? Why or why not?

E RESEARCH TOPIC

Are people's activities healthy or unhealthy? Find out by interviewing three people outside of class about their activities. Work in pairs.

1. Write at least five questions about healthy and unhealthy activities. Use the activities from the lists you made in Section 1B on page 132, and think of some more.

   Example questions: How often do you exercise?

   How often do you eat fattening foods?

   Do you smoke?

2. Now interview the people. One of you asks the questions. The other one writes down the answers.

3. Then report back to the class. Make sure you give the gender (male or female) and the age of each person you interviewed. Then discuss these questions.

   • What are some healthy activities and some unhealthy activities of the people you interviewed?

   • What health advice would you give to the people you interviewed?

Listening Task

Listen to your classmates' reports. Do you think more people are healthy or unhealthy? Why? Who do you think are healthier, men or women?

For Unit 9 Internet activities, visit the NorthStar Companion Website at
http://www.longman.com/northstar.

Endangered Languages

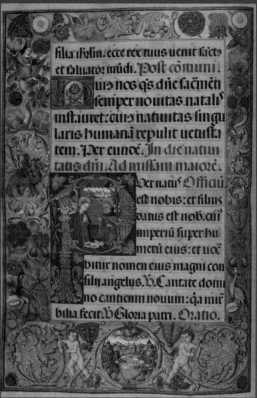

1 Focus on the Topic

A PREDICTING

Look at the pictures, and discuss these questions with the class.

1. Do you recognize the language in the picture on the left? What is it?

2. Do you recognize the language in the picture on the right? What is it?

3. Which language do people speak today?

4. What is a living language?

5. Read the title of the unit. What do you think it means?

B SHARING INFORMATION

Work with three other students. Discuss these questions.

1. What is your native language?

2. How many languages do you speak?

3. Do you speak the same language as your parents? grandparents?

4. What languages do you think your children will learn?

5. What is the official language of your country?

C PREPARING TO LISTEN

BACKGROUND

Take this short quiz. See what you know. When you are done, look at the list of facts below and check your answers.

1. How many languages are there in the world?
   a. less than 1,000
   b. between 1,000 and 5,000
   c. more than 5,000

2. What is an endangered language?
   a. a language children no longer learn
   b. a language adults no longer speak
   c. a language not many people speak

3. What percentage of languages could be dead by 2100?
   a. 50%
   b. 75%
   c. 90%

Facts about Languages

- There are over 6,000 languages in the world today.

- A dead language means people do not speak the language any more.

- Many languages are endangered. Children will soon stop learning them. Then only older people will speak them.

- Some languages are nearly extinct. Only a few old people speak them. When these speakers die, the language will be dead.

- Of the approximately 6,000 languages spoken in the world today, 90 percent could be dead by the year 2100.

VOCABULARY FOR COMPREHENSION

Read the sentences and guess the meanings of the underlined words.

1. Many languages are <u>endangered</u> and soon won't be spoken by anyone at all.

2. A <u>dead language</u> is a language that no one speaks anymore.

3. Many languages are <u>extinct</u>; they are gone and no one uses them anymore.

4. <u>Linguists</u> study languages, not to learn them but to understand the sounds, grammar, and meaning.

5. Some people prefer to live in their own <u>communities</u> among people who have something in common with them.

6. <u>Powerful</u> people have a strong effect on other people.

7. A long time ago, there were Native American languages spoken all over North America. Slowly, they have been <u>replaced</u> with English, and they are not spoken anymore.

8. In Europe, many people learn several languages, but their <u>native language</u> is the language spoken in the region they are from.

9. For Europeans, it is common to be <u>bilingual</u> and speak two languages. Many people even speak more than two languages.

10. Some native people try to <u>preserve</u> their languages, to keep them alive, by sending their children to language schools to learn their native languages.

Now match the words with their definitions.

__*f*__ 1. endangered language	**a.**	a group of people living together with shared, common interests
_____ 2. dead language	**b.**	to change one thing for another
_____ 3. extinct	**c.**	very strong
_____ 4. linguists	**d.**	speaking two languages
_____ 5. community	**e.**	a language belonging to the place of one's birth or to the original people of a place
_____ 6. powerful		
_____ 7. replace	**f.**	a language children will soon stop learning
_____ 8. native language	**g.**	people who study the science of language
_____ 9. bilingual	**h.**	no longer living or existing
_____ 10. preserve	**i.**	to save
	j.	a language people do not speak any more

2 Focus on Listening

A   LISTENING ONE: *Language Loss*

🎧 *Listen to the beginning of "Language Loss." Read each question. Then circle the correct answer.*

1. Where is the speaker?
   a. in a class   **b.** on TV   **c.** on the radio

2. What is the topic?
   a. languages   **b.** language and culture   **c.** endangered languages

3. What do you think the speaker might talk about? (*List three possibilities.*)

   _____

   _____

   _____

LISTENING FOR MAIN IDEAS

🎧 *Listen to the whole lecture on endangered and dead languages. Then read each statement and decide if it is true or false. Write **T** (true) or **F** (false) next to it.*

_____ 1. Linguists care about endangered languages because when a language dies, a culture can die, too.

_____ 2. Languages become endangered because children don't go to school.

_____ 3. Linguists try to preserve and save endangered languages.

LISTENING FOR DETAILS

🎧 *Listen to the lecture again. Then circle the correct answer to complete each statement.*

1. _____ is an example of a dead language.
   a. Spanish   **b.** Latin   **c.** Greek

2. The Manx lost their native _____.
   a. culture   **b.** traditions   **c.** language

3. According to the speaker, _____ are passed down through language.
   a. stories and poetry
   b. history and knowledge
   c. humor and culture

4. The government can make it _____
   to teach the language in school.
   a. required
   b. illegal
   c. difficult

5. Before _____, it was illegal to teach
   Hawaiian in public schools.
   a. 1997
   b. 1957
   c. 1987

6. Once there were _____ of Native
   American languages.
   a. a few
   b. hundreds
   c. thousands

7. In Greenland, students learn _____.
   a. only Danish
   b. Kalaallisut and Danish
   c. only Kalaallisut

Young Greenland girls

8. Linguists help create _____ programs where people can study endangered
   languages.
   a. interesting
   b. community
   c. unusual

*Now go back to Section 2A (question 3) on page 150. How many of your guesses did the
speaker discuss?*

REACTING TO THE LISTENING

 1 *Listen to two excerpts from the lecture. After listening to each excerpt, answer the
questions.*

Excerpt One

1. Does the student think that saving languages is important?

2. How do you know?

Excerpt Two

1. Does the student think that linguists should do something?

2. Does the student's attitude change during the lecture?

3. How do you know?

Discuss these questions with the class. Give your opinions.

1. Do you think preserving languages is important? Why or why not?

2. Why do you think some people want to preserve languages?

3. Why do you think some people don't want to preserve languages?

B LISTENING TWO: *My Life, My Language*

Listen to a woman talk about a new kind of language school. Then read each question and circle the correct answer.

1. Where does she live?
   a. New Zealand
   b. Greenland

2. What language did she learn in school?
   a. Maori
   b. English

3. What language did her grandparents speak?
   a. Maori
   b. English

4. How did she feel in her family?
   a. empty and different
   b. happy and excited

5. Where do her children go to school?
   a. elementary school
   b. language nests

6. How many language nests are there now?
   a. over 13,000
   b. over 700

7. What are two values the children learn?
   a. love and caring
   b. hope and sharing

8. Where do the adults meet?
   a. libraries
   b. neighborhood centers

Young Maori boys

C   LINKING LISTENINGS ONE AND TWO

Look at the chart. On the left are ideas from Listening One. For each idea, pick one or two examples from the list and write them in the chart. You can use the same example for different ideas. Then discuss your answers with another student.

List of Examples

children learn Maori stories
children are able to speak to their grandparents
children learn Maori values
children start school knowing Maori and English
Maori language nests
adults learn the Maori language

Ideas from Listening One	Examples from Listening Two
Preserving culture	*children learn Maori values*
Speaking more than one language	
Preserving language	

3 Focus on Vocabulary

1 *Work with another student. The following statements are wrong and need to be corrected. Read each statement, look at the underlined words, and discuss with your partner why the statement is wrong. Then correct the statement. You can change any word to make the statement correct.*

       People don't   *anymore*
1. ~~Children~~ ^speak <u>dead languages</u>^.

2. <u>Endangered languages</u> will probably survive a long time.

3. An <u>extinct</u> language is spoken by many people.

4. <u>Linguists</u> study cultures and places.

5. A <u>community</u> is a group of people who have nothing in common.

6. Sometimes the language of a less powerful community <u>replaces</u> the language of a more powerful community.

7. People who grow up in the United States speak Chinese as a <u>native language</u>.

8. Linguists want to <u>preserve</u> languages because they don't want others to learn them.

9. Linguists worry that endangered languages won't <u>disappear</u> and be forgotten.

10. Spanish is the <u>official language</u> of the United States.

2 *Work in a group of three students. Think about the information you learned in Listening One and Listening Two. Use words from the box to discuss the questions. Try to use all these words. You can use other words as well.*

communities	linguist
dead language	native language
disappear	official language
endangered language	preserve
extinct	replace

1. What does a linguist who is interested in endangered languages do?

2. Why are people concerned about endangered languages?

3. Do you think Maori language nests are important? Why or why not?

4. Why do languages become endangered or extinct?

5. Do you think a country should have more than one official language? Why or why not?

6. Is your native language or another language in your country endangered? What is being done to preserve it?

4 Focus on Speaking

A PRONUNCIATION: Using Contractions with *Will*

When you speak, use the contraction *'ll* for *will* and **won't** for *will not*.

 Listen to these examples:

When my children start school, **they'll** learn English.
My children **won't** forget Maori, because **I'll** speak it at home.

Use *will* after pronouns: *I'll, you'll, she'll, he'll, we'll, they'll.*

When the word before *will* ends in a consonant, pronounce it [l] and join it to the preceding word. The underlined words in the sentence below sound the same.

 Listen to this example:

Nick'll give me a nickel.

The contraction *-ll* is usually written only after pronouns. Even when the full form *will* is written, it is usually pronounced as a contraction.

WE WRITE: What will you do?
WE SAY: "Whattul" you do?

 1 *Listen to and repeat the sentences. Use contractions* **'ll** *and* **won't**.

1. When I have children, I'll make sure they speak Maori.

2. When they go to school, they'll study only English.

3. If you go to Greenland, you'll hear two languages.

4. If the language dies, the culture won't survive.

5. In 2100, there won't be as many languages as now.

6. In the future, many children won't speak the same languages as their grandparents.

2 *Work in pairs. Student A, ask one of the questions. Use the contraction **'ll** when you can. Student B, listen to the question, choose an answer, and read it aloud. Change roles after item 4.*

Student A	Student B
1. What will happen to many languages?	**a.** No, I won't stop speaking my language.
2. What will happen when the last native speaker dies?	**b.** They will disappear.
3. How will children learn the native language of their country?	**c.** They will go to language schools and speak with other people.
4. How will you preserve your native language?	**d.** Because my friends won't understand me.
5. Will you stop speaking your native language?	**e.** The language will die.
6. Why won't you speak your native language to your friends?	**f.** The culture will disappear.
7. What will happen to a culture if a language dies?	**g.** I will continue to use my native language.

B   STYLE: Giving Examples

Examples are used to explain a general statement.

General Statement

PROFESSOR: The government can make it illegal to teach the language in school.

Example

For example, before 1987, it was illegal to teach the Hawaiian language in Hawaii's public schools.

Here, the professor first makes a statement: He says that the teaching of language can be illegal. Then he gives a specific example of the Hawaiian language.

> **Giving Examples**
>
> There are several ways to give examples:
>
> **For instance,...**
>
> **For example,...**
>
> **An example of this is...**

Work in pairs. Student A, look at this page. Student B, go to page 165 and follow the instructions there.

Student A, ask the questions below. Student B will answer you based on the information given on his or her page.

Student A's Questions

1. Are Native American languages endangered?

2. Is the Maori language endangered?

3. Are the Maori trying to save their language?

4. Do some languages die slowly?

Now change roles. Student B asks you questions. Answer each question based on the information given below. Make sure you give an example. Use all three ways of giving an example.

Student A's Information

5. Twenty years ago, all the children in the Yupik Eskimo communities in Alaska spoke Yupik; today, the youngest speakers of Yupik in some of these communities are in their twenties, and the children speak only English.

6. Scottish Gaelic was spoken on Cape Breton Island, Nova Scotia, until the 1940s, but by the 1970s, children stopped learning the language.

7. In the past, the people of a country were responsible for saving their endangered language. Now, linguists and other interested people have started organizations to help preserve endangered languages.

8. Katherine Silva Saubel is the last living fluent speaker of one Native American language called Cahuilla (pronounced: ka-wee-a).

C GRAMMAR: Future with *Will*

1 *Read the following conversation. Underline the verbs. Then answer the questions that follow.*

A: What will happen to the language?

B: The language will disappear.

A: Will children stop learning the language?

B: Yes, they will.

a. What is the tense in each question above? How do you know?

b. Look at each verb after *will* in the conversation. What is its form?

Future with *Will*

1. Use *will* to ...

• Talk about general facts about the future.	Languages **will** die. Others **will** replace them.
• Make predictions about the future.	Linguists predict 90 percent of languages **will** be extinct in 100 years.

2. To form statements with *will* ...

• Use *will* plus the base form of the verb.	Maori children **will be** bilingual when they leave the language nests.
• Use the **contraction** of *will* (*'ll*) with pronouns in speaking.	**They'll** speak both Maori and English. **She'll** be able to speak with her grandparents.
• Do not use contractions in affirmative short answers.	A: Will they save their culture? B: Yes, they **will.**

3. To form a negative statement with *will* ...

• Use *will not* or *won't* plus the base form of the verb.	In Greenland, students are bilingual, so they *will not* lose their native language.
• Notice the contraction.	They *won't* lose their native language.
• Use *won't* in negative short answers.	A: Will they lose their language? B: No, they **won't.**

4. To form questions with *will* ...

• *yes/no* questions: use *will* + subject + base form of the verb	*Will* **we lose** the language?
• *wh-* questions: begin the question with a *wh-* word	*When* will **we learn** the language?

2 *Work with two other students. Read the questions. Make predictions. Write each student's answer and reason for their prediction.*

Questions	_____ name	_____ name	_____ name
1. Will your language disappear?			
2. Will your children learn more than one language?			
3. Will your children speak the same language as your grandparents?			
4. Will you stop speaking your native language?			
5. Will language change because of the Internet?			
6. Will new languages appear?			

D SPEAKING TOPICS

You're going to discuss the future of some endangered languages. Follow these steps.

1. Work with a partner. Look at the information about these endangered languages. Take turns asking and answering questions about the future of these languages. Use *will* and give examples to support your answers.

Example:

LANGUAGE:	*Mohawk*
LOCATION:	Ontario, Canada and New York, USA
NUMBER OF SPEAKERS:	About 3,000
LANGUAGE PROGRAMS:	Some programs in local schools and after school, but most children are not in these programs

A: Will Mohawk be a dead language soon?

B: Yes, I think it will. For example, there are some programs teaching Mohawk, but most children are not in these programs. Most Mohawk children don't learn their language, so they won't speak it later.

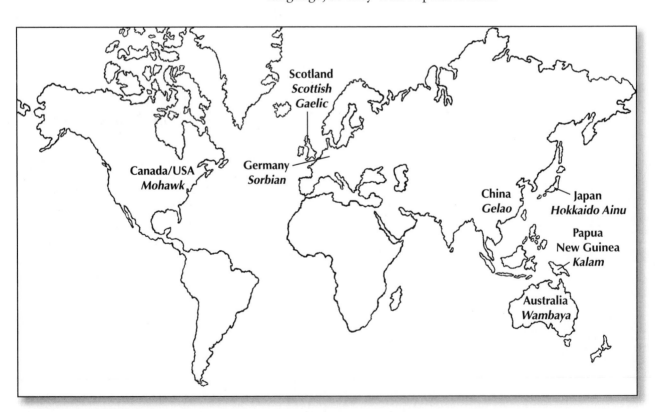

a. LANGUAGE: *Sorbian*
   LOCATION: Germany
   NUMBER OF SPEAKERS: About 60,000
   LANGUAGE PROGRAMS: Language instruction in some schools
                            Learned as a second language

b. LANGUAGE: *Hokkaido Ainu*
   LOCATION: Japan
   NUMBER OF SPEAKERS: Possibly 40
   LANGUAGE PROGRAMS: Some language programs, but young people are
                            not interested in it

c. LANGUAGE: *Kalam*
   LOCATION: Papua New Guinea
   NUMBER OF SPEAKERS: About 20,000
   LANGUAGE PROGRAMS: All children are learning it

d. LANGUAGE: *Wambaya*
   LOCATION: Australia
   NUMBER OF SPEAKERS: About 12 fluent people over 60 years old; some
                            people 35–40 years old know a little, but don't
                            speak it; no children speak it or are learning it
   LANGUAGE PROGRAMS: No language programs

e. LANGUAGE: *Gelao*
   LOCATION: China
   NUMBER OF SPEAKERS: About 3,000
   LANGUAGE PROGRAMS: No language programs

f. LANGUAGE: *Scottish Gaelic*
   LOCATION: Scotland
   NUMBER OF SPEAKERS: About 70,000
   LANGUAGE PROGRAMS: Bilingual programs in playgroups and school

2. Look at the information above. What do you think is the most endangered
language? Why? What could be done to save it? Tell your partner.

Listening Task

*Listen to your partner and fill out the chart below. Then work in a small group. Compare
your charts.*

Most endangered language	For what reasons?	What could be done?

E RESEARCH TOPIC

You're going to research an endangered language and culture. Follow these steps.

1. Go to the library or use the Internet. Find out about an endangered culture and language (like the ones listed below). Use the following questions to help you. Take notes.

Breton	Cornish	Navajo	Chamorro	Sonsorolese
Trumai	Sare	Alagwa	Rangi	Ugong

   a. What is the name of the endangered language?

   b. Where is the language spoken?

   c. How many people speak the language? How old are they?

   d. Is anything being done to preserve the language?

   e. Will this language survive?

2. Report to the class. Tell them about this language and about its future.

Listening Task

Listen to your classmates' reports. Which languages are the most endangered?

For Unit 10 Internet activities, visit the NorthStar Companion Website at http://www.longman.com/northstar.

Student Activities

3. Focus on Vocabulary. Exercise 1, page 77.

Student B, follow these instructions.

You and Student A, each have a crossword puzzle. You each have four words filled in. You each are missing four words. To complete the crossword puzzle, you need to know the words your partner has, and your partner needs to know the words you have.

Take turns reading the clues. For each clue, tell your partner the number and if it is across or down. Your partner will try to guess the word. Tell your partner if he or she is correct. When you guess the correct word, write it into the crossword puzzle.

Student B, listen to Student A read his or her clues. Try to guess the words. Use the following list to help you. When you have guessed correctly, write the word in your crossword puzzle.

block	illegal	ridiculous	save time
bother	legal	rude	suggestion

Student B, now read these clues to your partner. Student A will try to guess the word. If A is correct, say, "That's correct." If A made a mistake, say, "That's not correct."

1. *(down)* Many people called in to Terry's radio show to give their "ideas" about rude cell phone behavior. This is another word that means "idea."

2. *(down)* This word means "not allowed by law."

4. *(down)* One caller told about seeing a bus driver talking on a cell phone. The caller thought it was very silly. This is another word for "silly."

6. *(across)* To prevent something.

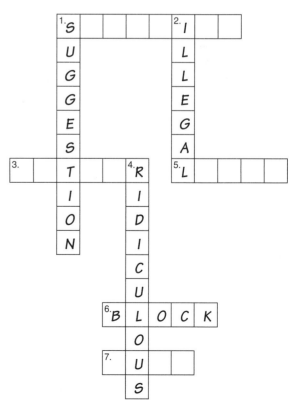

UNIT 8: An Ice Place to Stay

4B. Style. Exercise page 126.

Student B, you are staying at the Himalaya Inn in Katmandu, Nepal. Ask Student A polite questions to get the following information. Write the answers. If you don't know how to spell a word, ask Student A to spell it for you.

1. The location of an Indian restaurant: _____

2. The cost of a meal there: _____

3. The cost of a Japanese meal: _____

4. The hours of the post office on Saturday: _____

5. The hours of the bank on Sunday: _____

6. The cost to enter the Royal Palace: _____

Now change roles.

Student B, you are a clerk at the information desk of the Sunset Hotel in Los Angeles, California. Look at your list of information and answer your partner's requests.

THE SUNSET HOTEL
Los Angeles, California

Tourist Information

Local Restaurants

Hard Rock Cafe
Kind of food: American
Location: in Hollywood
Cost of a meal: about $30

The Dining Room
Kind of food: California style
Location: in Beverly Hills
Cost of a meal: about $50
children

Local Attractions

Universal Movie Studios Themepark
Location: Universal City
Hours: 10 A.M. to 6 P.M. daily
Cost: $45 for adults, $35 for children

Disneyland
Summer hours: Sunday–Friday, 8 A.M. to 11 P.M.
                        Saturday, 9 A.M. to 12 midnight
Cost of ticket: $45 for adults, $35 for

Tourist Office
Location: 685 Figueroa St.
Telephone: (213) 689-8822
Hours: Weekdays 8 A.M. to 5 P.M.
           Saturdays 8:30 A.M. to 5 P.M.

UNIT 10: Endangered Languages

4B. Style. Exercise page 157.

Student B, listen to Student A's questions. Answer each question based on the information below. Make sure you give an example. Use the three ways of giving an example.

Student B's Information

1. Once there were 100 Native American languages in California. Now 50 of these languages are dead and 7 have no fluent speakers.

2. In the early 1970s, there were about 64,000 Maori speakers in New Zealand. In 1995, there were about 10,000.

3. There are now over 700 language nests across New Zealand, which are teaching more than 100,000 Maori children their native tongue.

4. Iroquoian languages like Onondaga and Mohawk, spoken in upstate New York and parts of Canada, have been slowly dying for over 200 years.

Now change roles.

Student B, ask the following questions. Student A will answer you based on the information given on his or her page.

Student B's Questions

5. Do some languages die quickly?

6. Do children sometimes stop learning a language?

7. Do people sometimes try to save a language?

8. Do some languages have very few fluent speakers?

Grammar Book References

NorthStar: Listening and Speaking, Basic/Low Intermediate, Second Edition	Focus on Grammar: A Basic Course for Reference and Practice, Second Edition	Azar's Basic English Grammar, Second Edition
Unit 1 Descriptive Adjectives	**Unit 6** Descriptive Adjectives	**Chapter 1** Using *Be* and *Have*: 1-6 **Chapter 4** Nouns and Pronouns: 4-2 **Chapter 8** Nouns, Adjectives and Pronouns: 8-14
Unit 2 Simple Past Tense	**Unit 4** The Past Tense of *Be*; Past Time Markers **Unit 18** Simple Past Tense: Regular Verbs—Affirmative and Negative Statements **Unit 19** Simple Past Tense: Irregular Verbs—Affirmative and Negative Statements **Unit 20** Simple Past Tense: *Yes/No* and *Wh-* Questions	**Chapter 5** Expressing Past Time
Unit 3 Comparative Adjectives	**Unit 38** Comparative Form of Adjectives	**Chapter 9** Making Comparisons: 9-3
Unit 4 Simple Present Tense—*Wh-* Questions with *Do*	**Unit 15** Simple Present Tense: *Wh-* Questions	**Chapter 2** Expressing Present Time (1): 2-11, 2-12, 2-13
Unit 5 Verbs plus Gerunds and Infinitives	**Unit 27** Verbs plus Nouns, Gerunds, and Infinitives	

NorthStar: Listening and Speaking, Basic/Low Intermediate, Second Edition	Focus on Grammar: A Basic Course for Reference and Practice, Second Edition	Azar's Basic English Grammar, Second Edition
Unit 6 Adverbs and Expressions of Frequency	**Unit 25** Present and Present Progressive; *How often . . . ?*; Adverbs and Expressions of Frequency	**Chapter 2** Expressing Present Time (1): 2-2, 2-3
Unit 7 Count and Non-count Nouns	**Unit 33** Count and Non-count Nouns and Quantifiers	**Chapter 4** Nouns and Pronouns: 4-6, 4-8, 4-9, 4-12
Unit 8 *Can* and *Can't*	**Unit 35** *Can* and *Could* for Ability and Possibility; *May I, Can I,* and *Could I* for Polite Requests	**Chapter 7** Expressing Ability: 7-1, 7-2
Unit 9 *Should, Ought to,* and *Have to*	**Unit 42** *Should, Shouldn't, Ought to, Had better,* and *Had better not* **Unit 43** *Have to, Don't have to, Must, Mustn't*	**Chapter 10** Expressing Ideas with Verbs: 10-1, 10-3
Unit 10 Future with *Will*	**Unit 32** *Will* for the Future	**Chapter 6** Expressing Future Time: 6-5, 6-6

Audioscript

UNIT 1: Offbeat Jobs

2A. LISTENING ONE: *What's My Job?*

Host: Good afternoon everybody, and welcome to *What's My Job?*—the game show about offbeat jobs. I'm your host, Wayne Wonderful. Today's first contestant is Rita, a secretary from Chicago, Illinois.

Rita: Hi, Wayne. I'm so happy to be here! Hi, Mom. Hi, Dad. Hi, Joe. . . .

Host: OK, Rita. Let's get started. You're going to meet some people who will describe their jobs. Then you can ask three questions to guess each person's job. You can win $1,000 for each job you guess correctly. Are you ready? Let's welcome our first guest, Peter. OK, Peter, can you tell us a little about your job?

LISTENING FOR MAIN IDEAS

Host: Good afternoon everybody, and welcome to *What's My Job?*—the game show about offbeat jobs. I'm your host, Wayne Wonderful. Today's first contestant is Rita, a secretary from Chicago, Illinois.

Rita: Hi, Wayne. I'm so happy to be here! Hi, Mom. Hi, Dad. Hi, Joe. . . .

Host: OK, Rita. Let's get started. You're going to meet some people who will describe their jobs. Then you can ask three questions to guess each person's job. You can win $1,000 for each job you guess correctly. Are you ready? Let's welcome our first guest, Peter. OK, Peter, can you tell us a little about your job?

Peter: Sure, Wayne. At my job, I work with food. My work is very interesting because I can enjoy good food and I can be creative.

Host: That does sound interesting. OK Rita, go ahead and ask your three questions.

Rita: Do you work in a restaurant?

Peter: No, I don't.

Rita: Hmm . . . Do you work in a bakery?

Peter: No, I don't. I work in a factory.

Rita: A factory? Do you make food?

Peter: Yes, I help to make food.

Host: OK. That's three questions. Now Rita, can you guess Peter's job?

Rita: Hmm . . . Are you a chef?

Peter: No, I'm not a chef.

Host: Ah, sorry Rita. So tell us, Peter. What do you do?

Peter: I'm an ice-cream taster.

Rita: An ice-cream taster?

Peter: That's right. I work in an ice-cream factory. I make sure the ice cream tastes good. I also think of interesting new flavors to make.

Host: Gee, sounds like a difficult job, Peter. You taste ice cream all day and you get paid for it!

Peter: Yes, that's right. I'm lucky to have such a great job.

Host: Good for you. So tell us Peter, is there anything difficult about your job?

Peter: Well . . . I guess so . . . For one thing, I can't eat all the ice cream. Otherwise I'd get too full. I only taste a little bit of ice cream and then I have to spit it out.

Host: I see. Is there anything else that's difficult?

Peter: Let me think. Well, I have to be very careful to take care of my taste buds. For example, I can't eat spicy or hot foods.

Host: Really?

Peter: Yes, and I don't drink alcohol or coffee . . . And I don't smoke either. If I did those things, I might hurt my taste buds, and then I wouldn't be able to taste the ice cream very well.

Host: Wow. You do have to be careful.

Peter: Yes, I do. In fact, my taste buds are so important that they are covered by a one million-dollar insurance policy.

Host: One million dollars! You don't say!

Peter: That's right. You see, if I can't taste the ice cream, my company and I will lose a lot of money.

Host: Gee, you do have a very important job, Peter. So how did you get started as an ice-cream taster? Did you go to ice-cream tasting school?

Peter: Oh, no. My family has been in the ice-cream business for a long time. I've always wanted to work with ice cream, too.

Host: That's great, Peter. Thank you very much for being on the show, and keep up the good work! OK everybody, it's time for a commercial break. But, don't go away. We'll be right back with our next guest, on *What's My Job?*

LISTENING FOR DETAILS

(*Repeat Listening for Main Ideas.*)

REACTING TO THE LISTENING

Excerpt One

Rita: Hi, Wayne. I'm so happy to be here! Hi, Mom. Hi, Dad. Hi, Joe. . . .

Host: OK, Rita. Let's get started.

Excerpt Two

Peter: That's right. I work in an ice-cream factory. I make sure the ice cream tastes good. I also think of interesting new flavors to make.

Host: Gee, sounds like a difficult job, Peter. You taste ice cream all day and you get paid for it!

Peter: Yes, that's right. I'm lucky to have such a great job.

Excerpt Three

Host: So how did you get started as an ice-cream taster? Did you go to ice-cream tasting school?

Peter: Oh, no. My family has been in the ice-cream business for a long time. I've always wanted to work with ice-cream, too.

2B. LISTENING TWO: *More Offbeat Jobs*

Job Number 1

Young Man: I'm a window washer. I go high up in the air in a basket to reach the windows on tall office buildings, so I can wash them. I really like my job because I enjoy being outdoors. I like to breathe the fresh air and look at the beautiful views of the city. It's really relaxing. And I earn a high salary. But . . , My job is dangerous. I have to be very careful not to fall out of the basket, and I have to be careful not to drop things on people below. Window washing is a great job for me because I'm good with my hands, and I don't mind doing dangerous work. Even so, it was difficult for me to get started as a window washer. But now, I have my own business. It's great!

Job Number 2

Middle-aged Woman: I'm a professional shopper. I go shopping for people who are busy and don't have time to shop. People give me a shopping list and some money, and I do the shopping for them. I like my job because I love to shop and I really like to work with people. I'm also very good with money. My job is great, but it isn't that easy. I'm on my feet a lot, so my work is tiring. And it wasn't easy to get started as a shopper. I worked for many years as a salesclerk in a department store. Then I started to meet people who needed a shopper. When I had enough customers, I quit my job at the department store and started my own business.

4A. PRONUNCIATION

careful

creative

adventurous

animal trainer

salesclerk

professional shopper

good pay

Exercise 1

1. dangerous
2. important
3. relaxing
4. educated
5. artistic
6. patient
7. unusual
8. interesting

Exercise 2

1. private detective
2. window washer
3. high salary
4. taste buds
5. ice cream
6. spicy foods
7. department store

UNIT 2: A Piece of the Country in the City

2A. LISTENING ONE: *Community Gardens*

Reporter: Hi, I'm Laura Lee from WNYZ News Radio here in New York City. I'm standing in front of a community garden. Community gardens are gardens that many people make together. Each person uses a small area to plant flowers or vegetables. Together, they make a community garden. It's a nice way to have a little piece of the country in the city or the suburbs. In fact, there are over 700 community gardens in New York.

This garden started a few years ago when the city let people in this neighborhood use an empty lot to make a community garden. But now, the city wants to remove the garden. Let's go talk to someone and see what he thinks about it. Hello . . . How are you doing?

LISTENING FOR MAIN IDEAS

Reporter: Hi, I'm Laura Lee from WNYZ News Radio here in New York City. I'm standing in front of a community garden. Community gardens are gardens that many people make together. Each person uses a small area to plant flowers or vegetables. Together, they make a community garden. It's a nice way to have a little piece of the country in the city or the suburbs. In fact, there are over 700 community gardens in New York.

This garden started a few years ago when the city let people in this neighborhood use an empty lot to make a community garden. But now, the city wants to remove the garden. Let's go talk to someone and see what he thinks about it. Hello . . . How are you doing?

Man: Oh, hello.

Reporter: Hi, I'm a reporter from WNYZ News Radio. I understand the city wants to remove this garden. Is that correct?

Man: Yes, that's right. Can you believe it? After all this work we've done.

Reporter: You don't sound happy.

Man: I'm not. You see, ten years ago before we planted the garden, this was just an empty lot. The city gave us this empty lot to make a community garden. All the people in the neighborhood worked really hard. We planted *everything* you see . . . flowers, vegetables, trees. We worked together and made this beautiful community garden.

Reporter: The garden does make the neighborhood look nice.

Man: You bet it does. You should have seen this place before we planted the garden. It had garbage on it and people just hung around. We made it beautiful. Now, the city wants to remove all of this to build apartment buildings. I can't believe it.

Reporter: Well, we all know there are not enough apartments in New York . . . right?

Man: Yeah, I know it, too. But there are other empty lots in the city. They can build apartments there.

Reporter: Are there other reasons this garden is important?

Man: Sure. Before we planted the garden, we didn't have a place to enjoy nature. There isn't a lot of nature in the city, you know.

Reporter: Yes, I know what you mean.

Man: This neighborhood didn't have trees or flowers. People had no place to come and sit. You know, get together with their friends and talk or just relax. Children didn't have a place to play either. Now, there is a place for children to play and people to relax or meet their friends. We have a small part of the country in the city now and a place to enjoy nature.

Reporter: Hmm. It sounds like the garden is really good for the people in the neighborhood.

Man: Yeah, it is. Before we planted this garden, some people sold drugs here. They didn't have jobs and didn't know how to do anything. Then they joined this garden and learned how to grow food. Now, they sell vegetables, not drugs.

Reporter: So this garden taught people about plants and gave people jobs.

Man: Yeah. And another thing. There are people like me. I grew up in the country. My family grew all our food. When I moved to the city, I lived in an apartment building with no yard so I couldn't grow food anymore. In this community garden, I can grow vegetables again . . . And they taste great, much better than supermarket vegetables. Boy, I sure don't like those supermarket vegetables.

Reporter: I understand. I don't like them either. Well, thank you for telling us about this community garden.

Man: Thanks for coming out here.

Reporter: OK. Good luck. . . .

Man: Take care.

Reporter: So, community gardens really give people a small part of the country in the middle of the city. They also make the neighborhood a nicer place to live. Tomorrow night, we will find out what the city of New York plans to do about this garden. Until then, good night.

LISTENING FOR DETAILS

(Repeat Listening for Main Ideas.)

REACTING TO THE LISTENING

Excerpt One

Reporter: The garden does make the neighborhood look nice.

Man: You bet it does. You should have seen this place before we planted the garden. It had garbage on it and people just hung around. We made it beautiful. Now, the city wants to remove all of this to build apartment buildings. I can't believe it.

Except Two

Man: This neighborhood didn't have trees or flowers. People had no place to come and sit. You know, get together with their friends and talk or just relax. Children didn't have a place to play either. Now, there is a place for children to play and people to relax or meet their friends. We have a small part of the country in the city now and a place to enjoy nature.

2B. LISTENING TWO: *Let's Hear from Our Listeners*

Host: Good afternoon and welcome to *Talk of the Town.* I'm Juana Ramon. You know, community gardens are one kind of urban greening or urban beautification. Today, we want to hear from you, our listeners. What urban greening programs do you see in the city? Let's hear from our first caller. Hello. You're on the air.

Caller 1: Yeah, hi. About five years ago, all the neighbors in my neighborhood got together and planted trees—one tree in front of each house. Now, there are beautiful trees all along the street. The trees make the street shady and cool in the summer and they make the neighborhood green.

Host: That's a great way to make a city greener. OK. Let's hear from another caller. You're on the air.

Caller 2: Hi. Well, I live in a tall apartment building. There are no empty lots in my neighborhood and there aren't any trees. But we do have a really nice garden on our roof. I really enjoy going there to relax. We have small trees and flowers . . . It's really wonderful.

Host: Roof gardens. What a great idea! Why not plant a garden on top of a building! Let's hear from one more caller. Good afternoon . . . You're on the air.

Caller 3: Hi, yeah. Um, my company decided to help make the city clean and beautiful by picking up garbage along the highway. It's called "Adopt-a-Highway." Our company agrees to take care of one mile of the highway and pick up the garbage.

Host: Yes, I have seen the "Adopt-a-Highway" signs on the side of the road. That's another wonderful way to help keep cities green and beautiful. Well, that's about all the time we have this afternoon. Until next week, this is Juana Ramon saying good-bye.

4A. PRONUNCIATION

I wanted to work in the garden yesterday.

I looked at the garden this morning.

The children played in the park.

wanted	looked	played
visited	missed	lived
ended	watched	listened

Exercise 2

1. I worked in the community garden yesterday.
2. She planted some vegetables last week.
3. My children played on an empty lot near my home.
4. I walked on a beautiful tree-lined street today.
5. Last week, the city removed garbage from an empty lot.
6. Everyone liked the flowers in the community garden.
7. My family lived in the city last year.
8. They stayed in the garden until evening yesterday.
9. I wanted to visit the country last weekend.
10. We watched some children playing.

UNIT 3: A Penny Saved Is a Penny Earned

2A. LISTENING ONE: *A Barter Network*

Woman 1: Good morning, everyone. Let's get started . . . My name's Carol, and I'd like to welcome you to the City Barter Network. I'm glad you all could come to today's meeting. And I'm happy to see so many people interested in joining our network. There are a few things I'd like to do this morning.

LISTENING FOR MAIN IDEAS

Woman 1: Good morning, everyone. Let's get started . . . My name's Carol, and I'd like to welcome you to the City Barter Network. I'm glad you all could come to today's meeting. And I'm happy to see so many people interested in joining our network. There are a few things I'd like to do this morning. First, I want to tell you a little about bartering—what bartering is. Then I'll explain how you can barter in our network. Then, if you want to join, I'll sign you up as a member. Any questions? OK. Let's get started. First of all, does everyone know what bartering is?

Man 1: Bartering is trading stuff, right? Like, I trade my car for your computer, or something like that?

Woman 1: Well, that's one kind of bartering—trading one thing for another thing—but in our barter network, we only exchange services—things you can do for another person.

Man 1: Oh, I see.

Woman 1: Here's how it works. First, when you join the network, you sign your name on our member list and you list all of the services you can provide. Every member gets a copy of the list or they can read it on our website.

Man 2: So, what kinds of services do members provide?

Woman 1: Most members provide services that a lot of people need like cooking, cleaning, or fixing things. But some people provide more unusual services like taking photographs, tutoring, or even giving music lessons.

Woman 2: Music lessons?! So, do you think I could get piano lessons? I've always wanted to learn how to play the piano.

Woman 1: Yeah, sure.

Woman 2: Wow! That's great!

Woman 1: It sure is! But remember that when you barter, you need to *provide* a service before you can *get* one . . . So that brings me to the next step, how to barter. After you become a member, another member can ask you to provide a service, to do something for them. For every hour of work you do for someone, you earn one Time Dollar.

Man 1: So, you can earn money?

Woman 1: No, you can't. Time Dollars aren't *real* money. Each Time Dollar just represents one hour of time that you spend providing a service. Later, you can spend your Time Dollars to get a service from someone else.

Man 1: So all the members earn one Time Dollar per hour, no matter what kind of work they do?

Woman 1: That's right. In our network, everyone's time is equal. No service is more valuable than another one. Let me give you an example. A few weeks ago another member needed some help cleaning his house. I spent three hours cleaning his house, so I earned three Time Dollars. Then last week, my television broke and I needed to get it fixed. So I called another member who fixed it for me. He spent one hour fixing it, so I spent one Time Dollar. It was great! I saved money because I didn't need to pay anyone to fix it for me.

Man 1: I have a question . . . What if you don't know how to *do* anything? I mean I don't really have any skills . . .

Woman 2: Hmm . . . can you walk?

Man 1: Walk? Well, of course I can. . . .

Woman 2: Then you can do dog-walking! I need someone to take my dog for a walk when I'm not home. Why don't *you* do it? . . .

Man 1: Well, I suppose I . . .

Woman 1: Great! It looks like you're all ready to barter! But, let's get signed up first. Next, I'll pass out some forms . . .

LISTENING FOR DETAILS

(*Repeat Listening for Main Ideas.*)

REACTING TO THE LISTENING

Excerpt One

Man 1: Bartering is trading stuff, right? Like, I trade my car for your computer, or something like that?

Woman 1: Well, that's one kind of bartering—trading one thing for another thing—but in our barter network, we only exchange services—things you can do for another person.

Man 1: Oh, I see.

Excerpt Two

Woman 1: But some people provide more unusual services like taking photographs, tutoring, or even giving music lessons.

Woman 2: Music lessons?! So, do you think I could get piano lessons? I've always wanted to learn how to play the piano.

Woman 1: Yeah, sure.

Woman 2: Wow! That's great!

Excerpt Three

Man 1: I have a question . . . What if you don't know how to *do* anything? I mean I don't really have any skills . . .

Woman 2: Hmm . . . can you walk?

Man 1: Walk? Well, of course I can. . . .

2B. LISTENING TWO: *Saving Money*

Conversation One

A: What're you doing?

B: I'm buying a new camera.

A: On the computer?

B: Yeah, I like to shop on the Internet.

A: Oh, yeah?

B: Sure, Internet shopping is great because it's easy to compare prices, so you can save money. The camera I want costs $800 in the stores, but I found it on the Internet for only $600.

A: You got a good deal—you saved $200.

B: Yeah, and it's a lot easier than shopping in stores. You don't have to leave your house. You just send in your credit card information and they send the stuff to your house.

A: That's true—but I'd rather pay cash than use my credit card. And I don't like sending my credit card information over the Internet.

Conversation Two

A: I like your lamp. It's very unusual. Where did you get it?

B: You'll never believe it, but I bought it used at a thrift store.

A: A thrift store, huh?

B: Yeah, it was really cheap. I only paid five dollars for it. I saved at least fifty dollars buying it used instead of new.

A: That's great that you saved money, but I'd never buy anything used. I only like to buy new things.

Coversation Three

A: Hey, where are you going?

B: I'm going to the outlet center. I want to buy some new clothes.

A: Isn't that far away?

B: Yes, it is pretty far away. It's out in the suburbs.

A: So why go to the outlet center? Isn't it easier to shop at the department store near your house?

B: Yeah, it's true—the department stores are closer, and there are usually more salesclerks to help you, too. But the clothes at the outlet stores are a lot less expensive. Last time, I found a jacket for 50 percent off the regular price. I saved seventy-five dollars!

A: Seventy-five dollars! That's great!

B: So, how about coming with me?

A: Why not? Maybe I'll save some money!

4A. PRONUNCIATION

13	30
16	60
19	90

four dollars and twenty-nine cents	four twenty-nine
fifty-three dollars and ninety-nine cents	fifty-three ninety-nine

Exercise 1

1. 13
2. 40
3. 50
4. 16
5. 70
6. 18
7. 19

Exercise 3

1. $7.50
2. $83.25
3. $ 319.40
4. $16.99
5. $1,500

UNIT 4: At Your Service: Service Animals

2A. LISTENING ONE: *Kimba, the Hero Dog*

Steve: . . . so we can look forward to sunny skies and warm weather this weekend. Our next story is reported by Ann Lycoff. She is at the scene of a fire. Ann.

Ann: Thanks, Steve. I'm here at what was the scene of a fire. This house caught on fire this morning. Firefighters arrived quickly and everyone was safe. But it was a close call. You see, the woman who lives here, Mrs. Ravenscroft, is deaf. When the fire started, the fire alarm went off. Mrs. Ravenscroft couldn't hear the alarm. But Mrs. Ravenscroft is the owner of a special dog named Kimba. And thanks to her dog, Kimba, she's OK now.

LISTENING FOR MAIN IDEAS

Steve: . . . so we can look forward to sunny skies and warm weather this weekend. Our next story is reported by Ann Lycoff. She is at the scene of a fire. Ann.

Ann: Thanks, Steve. I'm here at what was the scene of a fire. This house caught on fire this morning. Firefighters arrived quickly and everyone was safe. But it was a close call. You see, the woman who lives here, Mrs. Ravenscroft, is deaf. When the fire started, the fire alarm went off. Mrs. Ravenscroft couldn't hear the alarm. But Mrs. Ravenscroft is the owner of a special dog named Kimba. And thanks to her dog, Kimba, she's OK now.

Steve: So what happened, Ann?

Ann: Well, the fire started in the kitchen. Mrs. Ravenscroft was in the living room and did not hear the alarm. Kimba did hear the alarm and started running up and down the hall from the kitchen to the living room. Mrs. Ravenscroft saw the dog running and knew something was wrong. Mrs. Ravenscroft went to the kitchen and saw the fire. Flames were already three feet high! She immediately called 911 and the fire department came. Without the dog, she would not have known there was an alarm. Kimba saved Mrs. Ravenscroft's life. Mrs. Ravenscroft is very lucky. As you might guess, this is not just any dog. This is a special dog. Kimba is a hearing dog.

Steve: Huh. A hearing dog. What do hearing dogs do, Ann?

Ann: Well, hearing dogs are specially trained to assist deaf people. Hearing dogs tell deaf people about many different sounds, for example, the doorbell ringing, a baby crying, a fire alarm or the telephone ringing, and many more sounds, too. Hearing dogs go to special schools where they are trained how to tell deaf people about important sounds.

Steve: How do hearing dogs do it? How do they tell people about sounds?

Ann: Well, when the dog hears a sound, for example the doorbell, the dog first goes to the deaf person. The dog touches the deaf person to get their attention and then the deaf person knows the dog is trying to tell them something. Next, the dog goes to the sound, in this example, the door. The deaf person then knows that someone is ringing the doorbell or knocking on the door.

Steve: Where do deaf people use their hearing dogs?

Ann: Deaf people use hearing dogs in their homes of course, but sounds are everywhere—at work, on the bus, or on the street. So, deaf people bring their dogs with them everywhere they go. Also, hearing dogs can go into all public places, such as restaurants and stores. Basically, a hearing dog can go to work, on the bus, and out to dinner, too!

Steve: Really! Interesting.

Ann: Yes, it really is. So, Mrs. Ravenscroft didn't hear the alarm, but her companion and hearing dog, Kimba, did. Before the fire, Mrs. Ravenscroft called Kimba her personal hearing dog. Now, Mrs. Ravenscroft says Kimba is her personal hero dog because Kimba saved her life! So, tonight our story has a happy ending and everyone is safe! Back to you, Steve.

Steve: Thank you, Ann. And that's the news for this evening. Until tomorrow . . . Good night.

LISTENING FOR DETAILS

(*Repeat Listening for Main Ideas.*)

REACTING TO THE LISTENING

Excerpt One

Ann: Kimba saved Mrs. Ravenscroft's life. Mrs. Ravenscroft is very lucky. As you might guess, this is not just any dog. This is a special dog. Kimba is a hearing dog.

Steve: Huh. A hearing dog. What do hearing dogs do, Ann?

Excerpt Two

Ann: Basically, a hearing dog can go to work, on the bus, and out to dinner, too!

Steve: Really! Interesting.

2B. LISTENING TWO: *Do People Help Animals, Too?*

Man: Good morning, honey.

Woman: Hi, dear.

Man: Anything interesting in the paper today?

Woman: Yes. Listen to this . . . "Bandit, a six-month-old dog, is safe and happy tonight . . ."

Man: Is this another dog story because I really don't want to hear . . .

Woman: No, no, no. Just listen . . . Bandit, a young, curious dog, wandered off from his home last night and it seems he fell into an open sewer pipe. The sewer pipes on the street were being repaired. I guess he couldn't get out—he got stuck inside. When he didn't come home, his owners walked all over the neighborhood calling his name. Bandit heard his owners calling his name and got their attention by crying. Finally, his owners figured out where he was. They immediately called a company who came out and was able to save the poor dog. So tonight, he's safe at home again with his owners. What a lucky dog, don't you think?

Man: Yeah, yeah. So, a dog got lost and someone saved him.

Woman: It says here that the company usually charges about ten thousand dollars for the work they did. But they were so happy that the dog was safe, they did the work for free! Isn't that great!

Man: Well, that's a good use of money. Ten thousand dollars . . . I could do a lot with ten thousand dollars . . .

Woman: Honey—what about the poor dog? They couldn't just leave him there. He would die . . .

Man: It's a dog!

Woman: Right. . . .

4A. PRONUNCIATION

What do service animals do?

What does a hearing dog do?

Where do hearing dogs go ?

Exercise 1

1. What do service animals do?

2. What do hearing dogs do?

3. Where do deaf people use hearing dogs?

4. Why do deaf people use hearing dogs?

5. What do you think about hearing dogs?

UNIT 5: "Celletiquette"

2A. LISTENING ONE: *Everyone Has an Opinion*

Terry: Goooood morning! I'm Terry your host of *Terry Talks to the Town*. You know, cell phones have become very popular. What do you think of cell phones: Do you like them or do you think there're some problems with cell phones? Call me at 555-5555. Oh, here's our first caller—Hello, this is Terry and you're on the air.

LISTENING FOR MAIN IDEAS

Terry: Goooood morning! I'm Terry your host of *Terry Talks to the Town*. You know, cell phones have become very popular. What do you think of cell phones: Do you like them or do you think there're some problems with cell phones? Call me at 555-5555. Oh, here's our first caller—Hello, this is Terry and you're on the air.

Caller 1: Yeah, hi, um . . . let's see . . . cell phones . . . uh . . . yeah. I think they're great. I like using cell phones. In fact, I'm using one right now.

Terry: That wasn't a horn honking, was it?

Caller 1: Uh, yeah, it was . . . I'm driving . . . to work . . . I get a lot of work done in my car . . . I can't imagine not having my cell phone. It's very convenient. I hate to stop and use a pay phone. My cell phone saves me a lot of time.

Terry: So you're one of those people who talks and drives . . . hmm. OK, well thanks for calling. Wow—look at all those calls coming in . . . Hello, you're on the air.

Caller 2: That is exactly what I am talking about.

Terry: Uhh . . . sorry. What are you talking about?

Caller 2: Those people who drive and talk. They're talking when they should be paying attention. It's distracting. I almost got hit by a car and when I saw the driver, she was talking on her cell phone. Didn't even see me. That bothers me! People need to be more careful. It's their responsibility!

Terry: Yeah, and they drive too slowly, too . . . Have you noticed that?

Caller 2: I sure have. I can't stand it!.

Terry: . . . and where are you calling from?

Caller 2: Um . . . well . . . I'm standing in line to get a cup of coffee.

Terry: I see. So you're in a restaurant?

Caller 2: Yeah . . .

Terry: OK, thanks for your call. Oh, look at those lights! Hello, you're on the air.

Caller 3: OK, she's the problem. I don't mind people using cell phones in general, but when you go to a restaurant or out to the movies, turn off the cell phone.

Terry: I see . . . so cell phones in public places are rude.

Caller 3: They sure are. I don't want to hear cell phones ringing or overhear people having private conversations. Have a private conversation in private—you know? It's just common courtesy.

Terry: Right . . .

Caller 3: And I don't want to hear those silly ringing sounds either. I heard someone's phone ring while I was watching a movie in the theater.

Terry: Oh, gosh . . .

Caller 3: The guy answered the phone, and had a conversation—during the movie! Now that's ridiculous.

Terry: It sure is. All right. Thanks for calling. Next caller. What do you have to say?

Caller 4: Hi, um, I work nights, and I have to walk from my office to the car and drive a long way home . . . I love having a cell phone because I feel safe. If my car breaks down, I know I can call for help.

Terry: Right. Safety. That's a good point. One more caller. Hello?

Caller 5: Well, I am tired of all this talk about where and when I can use a cell phone . . . I don't know. I think I have the right to use my phone where and when I want to. No one can tell me not to. We don't have any laws about cell phone use.

Terry: Well, actually several states in the United States are passing laws now about driving and talking . . . And several countries now require drivers to use "hands-free devices" while driving . . . It's illegal to drive and talk without one.

Caller 5: Well, my state doesn't have a law.

Terry: Not yet anyway . . . OK, well, we sure have heard a lot of strong feelings about cell phones. Thanks for all your calls . . . Let's take a break for a commercial.

LISTENING FOR DETAILS

(*Repeat Listening One.*)

REACTING TO THE LISTENING

Excerpt One

Terry: That wasn't a horn honking, was it?

Caller 1: Uh, yeah, it was . . . I'm driving . . . to work . . . I get a lot of work done in my car . . . I can't imagine not having my cell phone. It's very convenient. I hate to stop and use a pay phone. My cell phone saves me a lot of time.

Terry: So you're one of those people who talks and drives . . . hmm. OK, well thanks for calling.

Excerpt Two

Terry: . . . and where are you calling from?

Caller 2: Um . . . well . . . I'm standing in line to get a cup of coffee.

Terry: I see. So you're in a restaurant?

Caller 2: Yeah . . .

2B. LISTENING TWO: *Our Listeners Write*

Terry: Welcome back to *Terry Talks to the Town*. Last week we heard from listeners about rude cell phone behavior. Well, I got several e-mails from listeners with suggestions. Let me read you three of them.

E-mail one is from Mark in Los Angeles, California.

"Dear Terry, I wanted to share some information about something called a jamming device. The device blocks the cell phone signal so your phone doesn't work. The good thing is people don't have to remember to turn off their phones at the movies or at a museum. The bad thing is that many people feel it's not right for someone else to control their phone. They are legal in some countries, but still illegal in most."

E-mail two is from Mary in White Plains, New York.

"Hi, Terry. I think theaters and restaurants should just put up a sign that says, 'please turn off your cell phone.' It seems the best way to me. I think a sign is all we need to control rude cell phone behavior. People should be responsible and polite. I also heard about another great idea called 'quiet cars'—cars on trains where you can't use your phone. I think it's good because you know if you sit there, it'll be quiet. These seem like two really good solutions to me."

E-mail three is from Alan in Seattle, Washington.

"Terry, I think we need laws about cell phones and driving. I think it should be illegal because it's really dangerous. Unfortunately, people can't control their own behavior, or don't have the common courtesy to do it themselves, so we need laws."

Well, I want to thank those of you who wrote in with your suggestions. They are all great ideas! Thanks!

4A. PRONUNCIATION

I hate to leave.

And I'd love to stay.

But I have to go.

Exercise 1

I'm going to call you on my cell phone

to see what you want to do

to make a plan

for later on

to meet and visit with you

we can meet to go to the store

or meet to see a movie

or meet to hang out and talk

and just spend a nice day together!

Exercise 2

1. a. I have a right to use my cell phone.

   b. I have the right to watch the movie in peace.

2. a. I hate to listen to your private conversations.

   b. I hate to use pay phones. They are too expensive.

3. a. I like to talk to my friends on the phone all day.

   b. I like to talk to my friends in a restaurant.

4. a. I like to drive and talk on the phone; it saves time.

   b. I like to feel safe when I drive. I like to know all drivers are watching the road!

UNIT 6: Is it Women's Work?

2A. LISTENING ONE: *Who's Taking Care of the Children?*

Host: Good afternoon, I'm Julie Jones. Welcome to *The Julie Jones Show*. Today, the topic is child care. As you know, in the United States, most parents of young children work and need to use child care. In fact, more than 50 percent of families with children in the United States *pay* for child care. Some families choose to hire a nanny to take care of the children. Today, we have a nanny here to tell us about the job. Let's welcome our nanny . . .

LISTENING FOR MAIN IDEAS

Host: Good afternoon, I'm Julie Jones. Welcome to *The Julie Jones Show*. Today, the topic is child care. As you know, in the United States, most parents of young children work and need to use child care. In fact, more than 50 percent of families with children in the United States *pay* for child care. Some families choose to hire a nanny to take care of the children. Today, we have a nanny here to tell us about the job. Let's welcome our nanny . . .

Man: Hello.

Host: Well, hello . . . And welcome to the show. You are an *unusual* nanny, aren't you?

Man: Unusual? Well . . . Yes, as you can see, I am a *male* nanny—or as some people say—a *manny*.

Host: A manny, eh? So tell me . . . Does a male nanny, or manny, do the same things as a female nanny?

Man: Well, yes, of course. A nanny's job, male or female, is to take care of children in a family's home. Nannies usually live with a family, but not always. And nannies often do household chores, like cooking and cleaning, too.

Host: I see, but a nanny is not a typical job for a man. I mean, it's a little unusual for a man to take care of children and do household chores, isn't it?

Man: Yeah, that's true. Most nannies are women—less than 5 percent of the nannies in the United States are men, but more men are starting to work as nannies these days.

Host: Hmm . . . I see . . . So, how exactly did *you* decide to become a nanny?

Man: Well, I've always really liked children. I enjoy taking care of them and playing with them. And I enjoy doing household chores, too. It's a good job for me.

Host: Really? So you like doing household chores? Great . . . But how did you learn to be a nanny? Do you have training?

Man: Yes, I do have training. I went to a special school that trains nannies. I studied about children and child care in my classes.

Host: I see . . . So . . . Was it easy for you to find work as a nanny?

Man: Well, no. To tell you the truth, it wasn't easy. A lot of people just don't think men can take care of children. They think child care is a woman's job. So, at first, many parents didn't want to give me a job because I'm a man. But then finally, I saw an ad for just the kind of job I wanted, so I applied and I got the job!

Host: I see. Were the parents looking for a *male* nanny?

Man: No, they weren't. First, I met the mother, and she was very surprised. I was the only man who applied for the job. But she liked me—and she has two boys. She thought they would like to have a male nanny . . . and she was right!

Host: So, the children like you?

Man: Yeah, we get along really well! The boys *like* having a male nanny. I like the same things they do—like sports and computers. I'm like a friend to them.

Host: So the mother hired you as a nanny. What did her husband think?

Man: Well . . . At first, her husband didn't like the idea. He thought only women could take care of children. And he didn't like having another man living in the house. You know . . . Sometimes he worked late and I was home . . . alone . . . with his wife. I think a lot of men might worry . . .

Host: So what happened?

Man: Well, her husband and I got to know each other and he saw that his children really liked me. He saw I was a good child-care worker and this, after all, is what's important.

Host: Well, *I* learned something today . . . that a man can be a nanny, and a good one, too. Thank you very much for coming, and until next week . . . This is Julie Jones saying good-bye.

LISTENING FOR DETAILS

(*Repeat Listening for Main Ideas.*)

REACTING TO THE LISTENING

Excerpt One

Host: Today, we have a nanny here to tell us about the job. Let's welcome our nanny . . .

Man: Hello.

Host: Well, hello . . . And welcome to the show. You are an *unusual* nanny, aren't you?

Excerpt Two

Man: Well, I've always really liked children. I enjoy taking care of them and playing with them. And I enjoy doing household chores, too. It's a good job for me.

Host: Really? So you like doing household chores? Great . . .

Excerpt Three

Host: So the mother hired you as a nanny. What did her husband think?

Man: Well . . . At first, her husband didn't like the idea. He thought only women could take care of children. And he didn't like having another man living in the house. You know . . . Sometimes he worked late and I was home . . . alone . . . with his wife. I think a lot of men might worry . . .

2B. LISTENING TWO: *Who is Right for the Job?*

Conversation 1

Woman: So, Joe. I heard your sister decided to join the fire department. What do you think about that?

Man: Well, I don't know. Most firefighters are men. I don't think women should be firefighters. It's really a man's job. You have to be strong.

Woman: Strong, huh. Don't you think women can be strong?

Man: No, not like a man.

Woman: Oh, I see.

Conversation 2

Man: My six-year-old daughter just started elementary school. I met her new teacher yesterday.

Woman: That's great. Did you like her?

Man: Oh, yes. I liked *him* a lot.

Woman: Oh, her teacher's a *man*—sorry.

Man: Oh, that's OK. I know teachers are usually women. But more men are starting to teach children these days. I think it's great. I think children should have both men and women as teachers.

Woman: You think so?

Man: Yeah, I think children should have men and women as role models at school. And boys need to know they can be teachers when they grow up, too.

Woman: That's a good point.

Conversation 3

Woman: My car broke down yesterday. I need to get it fixed.

Man: Really? I have a good mechanic. Would you like me to give you her name?

Woman: *Her* name? Your mechanic's a woman?

Man: Yeah, do you have a problem with that?

Woman: Uh . . . No . . . Not at all. I was just surprised. Women rarely work as mechanics, you know. Is she good at fixing cars? Does she have training?

Man: Of course!

Woman: Great! If she can do the job, that's all I need!

4A. PRONUNCIATION

Man: I enjoy doing housework.

Woman: Really?

Man: I was home alone with his wife.

Woman: And? . . .

Man: Well, her husband was worried.

Woman: I'm going to the post office now.

Man: Where?

Woman: To the post office.

Man: More men are working as nannies these days.

Woman: Hmm . . .

Woman: Was is easy for you to find work as a nanny?

Man: Well . . .

Exercise 1

1. **Woman:** I want to go to an all-women's college.
   Man: Really.
   Woman: Yeah, I think I'd like it.
2. **Man:** You know, I run thirty miles every day.
   Woman: Really.
   Man: Really . . . I do!
3. **Woman:** I need some help.
   Man: OK.
   Woman: Well . . . I need you to . . .

4. **Man:** I want to ask you something.
   Woman: Well . . .
5. **Woman:** Could you come over here?
   Man: Hmm . . .
   Woman: I said, could you come over here, please.
6. **Woman:** Do you want to go to the city or to the country?
   Man: Hmm . . .

UNIT 7: Good-Mood Foods

2A. LISTENING ONE: *Would You Like to Be on the Radio?*

Larry: Mmm, it tastes delicious. What's in it?

Dan: Well, thanks. I hope it works. I'll try anything.

Larry: On the radio? No, thanks.

Dan: Oh, my girlfriend just left me, and now I'm all alone.

Barbara: Are you kidding?! I'm in a big hurry. I don't have time for this!

LISTENING FOR MAIN IDEAS

Host: Good afternoon and welcome to *Street Talk*, the radio show where we talk to people on the street. I'm your host, Marty Moore, the *Street Talk* guy. Today, I'm here on Market Street talking to people about food. Did you know that eating some foods can actually change your moods? That's right! Some doctors say that if you're in a bad mood, you can eat a certain food and the food will make you feel better. So let's talk to some people and see what *they* think about food and moods. Here's someone now. Hi. I'm Marty Moore, the *Street Talk* guy. What's your name?

Larry: Me? My name's Larry. Why . . .

Host: Nice to meet you, Larry. Would you like to be on the radio?

Larry: On the radio? No, thanks. I think I'm too nervous for that.

Host: Oh, don't be nervous. Here, have some of this soup. It will help you relax.

Larry: Soup? Mmm, it smells delicious. What's in it?

Host: It's made with chili peppers.

Larry: Wow! That's hot!

Host: Oh, don't worry. Soon you'll feel better. You see, chili peppers have something in them that makes your mouth feel very hot right after you eat them. But they will also help you to relax. The more chili peppers you eat, the more relaxed you will feel.

Larry: I sure hope you're right!

Host: OK, on to the next person. Hi, I'm Marty Moore. What's your name?

Dan: I'm Dan.

Host: Gosh Dan, you look *really* unhappy. What's wrong?

Dan: Oh, my girlfriend just left me, and now I'm all alone. I feel miserable!

Host: Gee, I'm sorry to hear that. Maybe I can help you feel better. Here. Eat some of these chocolate chip cookies. You see, chocolate has something in it that makes you feel more upbeat. Some people even say chocolate can make you feel like you're in love!

Dan: In love? Really?

Host: Yes, and cookies are also made with wheat flour. Wheat can help you to relax and feel more upbeat, too.

Dan: Well, thanks. I hope it works. I'll try anything.

Host: Good luck. OK, let's talk to someone else . . . Hello. What's your name?

Barbara: My name? I'm Barbara. Who wants to know anyway?

Host: Well, I'm Marty Moore, the *Street Talk* guy. Would you like to be on the radio?

Barbara: Are you kidding?! I'm in a big hurry. I don't have time for this!

Host: Wow! You're in a bad mood. What's the matter?

Barbara: Sorry, but I'm really stressed! I'm late for work, and I'm still waiting for the bus! I hope it gets here soon. I have a lot of work to do, and my boss is going to be angry!

Host: Here, I've got just what you need. Eat this turkey sandwich, and drink this glass of orange juice.

Barbara: A turkey sandwich and orange juice? Are you crazy? I need a bus, not food!

Host: Hey, don't be so irritable. I'm just trying to help. You see, turkey can help you to feel more energetic so you can do all of your work and feel less stressed. And the vitamin C in your orange juice can also help you to feel more energetic. It can even help you to feel more upbeat so you won't be so irritable.

Barbara: Thanks anyway, but I don't have time for food. I have to get to work!

Host: Well, our time's up for today. This is Marty, the *Street Talk* guy, saying good-bye for now. And don't forget—eat the right foods, and stay in a good mood.

LISTENING FOR DETAILS

(Repeat Listening for Main Ideas.)

REACTING TO THE LISTENING

Excerpt One

Host: Oh, don't be nervous. Here, have some of this soup. It will help you relax.

Larry: Soup? Mmm, it smells delicious. What's in it?

Host: It's made with chili peppers.

Larry: Wow! That's hot!

Excerpt Two

Barbara: . . . I'm late for work, and I'm still waiting for the bus! I hope it gets here soon. I have a lot of work to do, and my boss is going to be angry!

Host: Here, I've got just what you need. Eat this turkey sandwich, and drink this glass of orange juice.

Barbara: A turkey sandwich and orange juice? Are you crazy? I need a bus, not food!

2B. LISTENING TWO: *What's the Matter?*

Narrator: What's the matter, Kate?

Kate: Oh, boy. Tomorrow's the big day. I'm getting married! I'm excited, but I'm really nervous, too. I hope I'm not making a mistake! I hope nothing goes wrong at the wedding!

Narrator: What's the matter, Derek?

Derek: Oh, my gosh, I'm totally stressed out. I have so much to do! I have to stay late at my job tonight to finish my work. Then I have to go to my son's school. He's in a play. I hope I can get there on time!

Narrator: What's the matter with Jane?

Jane: Hello? . . . What? No, he doesn't live here. You have the wrong number!

Ooooh, I hate it when people call and wake me up when I'm sleeping! And it really irritates me when it's a wrong number! How can people be so rude! Now I'll never get back to sleep!

Narrator: What's the matter, Jeff?

Jeff: I can't believe I just failed *another* math test. How stupid of me! And I needed a good grade on this test to pass the class . . . I feel miserable. What am I going to do?

4A. PRONUNCIATION

Exercise 1

I read a good book about mood foods.

Exercise 2

1. soon	9. would
2. look	10. cookies
3. cool	11. news
4. cook	12. food
5. soup	13. juice
6. Luke	14. book
7. too	15. noon
8. could	16. fruit

Exercise 4

1. a good cook	5. It's too soon.
2. fruit juice	6. good news
3. good soup	7. Cook the fruit.
4. Look at Luke.	8. Cool the soup.

UNIT 8: An Ice Place to Stay

2A. LISTENING ONE: *An Unusual Vacation*

Recorded Voice: Thank you for calling the Swedish travel telephone hotline. We have information about transportation, lodging, and tourist activities in Sweden. For information about transportation, press 1. For lodging, press 2, and for tourist activities, press 3.

(tone)

You've pressed 2 for information about lodging in Sweden. To hear more about campsites, press 1. For youth hostels, press 2. For small inns, press 3. For large hotels, press 4, and for information about a special hotel in Sweden, press 5.

(tone)

You've pressed 5 for a special hotel in Sweden. If you'd like to hear recorded information about the hotel, press 1. If you'd like to talk with a representative, press 2.

(tone)

You've pressed 2. Please hold . . .

LISTENING FOR MAIN IDEAS

Recorded Voice: Thank you for calling the Swedish travel telephone hotline. We have information about transportation, lodging, and tourist activities in Sweden. For information about transportation, press 1. For lodging, press 2, and for tourist activities, press 3.

You've pressed 2 for information about lodging in Sweden. To hear more about campsites, press 1. For youth hostels, press 2. For small inns, press 3. For large hotels, press 4, and for information about a special hotel in Sweden, press 5.

You've pressed 5 for a special hotel in Sweden. If you'd like to hear recorded information about the hotel, press 1. If you'd like to talk with a representative, press 2.

You've pressed 2. Please hold . . .

Woman: Hello. May I help you?

Man: Yes. Could you please tell me more about the special hotel in Sweden?

Woman: Certainly. That hotel is the Ice Hotel. It's located in a small town in Swedish Lapland, inside the Arctic Circle.

Man: I see.

Woman: When would you like to go?

Man: Well, I am looking for a winter vacation.

Woman: Perfect! In fact, you can't go any other time of year because it's only open in the winter. That's because it's made of ice and snow!

Man: Ice and snow?

Woman: Yes! You see, the Ice Hotel is built every November when the weather is cold. Then in the spring, it turns into water when the weather gets warm.

Man: It melts?

Woman: Of course! It's made of ice and snow! Would you like to hear more?

Man: Uh, yeah, I guess so . . .

Woman: Well, if you're adventurous and looking for an unusual vacation, the Ice Hotel is an interesting place to stay.

Man: Adventurous . . . what do you mean?

Woman: Well, the weather is very cold there in the winter. It's sometimes 40 degrees below freezing. Also, in the winter, the days are very short—there are sometimes only three hours of sunlight.

Man: Three hours? What can I do in three hours of sunlight?

Woman: Well, first, let me tell you about the hotel. The Ice Hotel has guest rooms for about 100 visitors to stay each night. The guest rooms all have tall beds made of snow, but there are no doors on the rooms. There aren't bathrooms either. If you need to use the bathroom, you can go to the nearby inn. There also aren't any closets for your clothes. Remember, the Ice Hotel is made of ice and snow, so the rooms are always very cold. To stay warm at night, you sleep in a very warm sleeping bag covered with reindeer furs. And don't forget to wear your hat to keep your ears warm!

Man: And the three hours of sunlight? What can I do in three hours of sunlight?

Woman: Well, there are some other rooms to visit at the hotel. For entertainment, you can look at some paintings in the hotel's art gallery. The Ice Hotel also has a small church, and some guests even get married there.

Man: Well, I'm not planning to get married!

Woman: Also, there are outdoor activities you can do near the Ice Hotel. If you enjoy outdoor winter activities, you can go cross-country skiing or snowshoeing. The exercise will warm you up quickly! You may also want to try dogsledding or snowmobiling. You can enjoy the ride and the beautiful arctic scenery.

Man: Huh. That all sounds very interesting. And could you tell me how much it costs?

Woman: Certainly. A room costs about $150 a night.

Man: Well, that's a lot of money, but for an interesting vacation, I guess it's worth it!

Woman: Yes, I think so, too. Is there anything else?

Man: Um, no. Thanks.

Woman: No problem. We hope you come to Sweden and visit the Ice Hotel. If you are looking for an unusual trip, we think you'll agree it's a nice place to stay!

Man: Bye!

LISTENING FOR DETAILS

(Repeat Listening for Main Ideas.)

REACTING TO THE LISTENING

Excerpt One

Man: Well, I am looking for a winter vacation.

Woman: Perfect! In fact, you can't go any other time of year because it's only open in the winter. That's because it's made of ice and snow!

Man: Ice and snow?

Excerpt Two

Woman: Well, the weather is very cold there in the winter. It's sometimes 40 degrees below freezing. Also, in the winter, the days are very short—there are sometimes only three hours of sunlight.

Man: Three hours? What can I do in three hours of sunlight?

2B. LISTENING TWO: *Vacations around the World*

Vacation Number 1

This travel package takes you to sunny southern California. Visit the world famous Disneyland amusement park and have the time of your life! When you aren't having fun at Disneyland, you can go sightseeing and take a tour of Hollywood. Maybe you'll even see some movie stars! You can also go shopping in Los Angeles or visit the art museums. Price includes four nights lodging at the Disneyland Hotel and bus tours of all the sights. Travel anytime!

Vacation Number 2

This tour is for the adventurous traveler who loves the outdoors. Go hiking through the Himalayan Mountains of Nepal, and go swimming in the rivers. Enjoy the beautiful views. On this trip, you will sleep outdoors in a campsite and meet other travelers from all over the world. You must be healthy for this vacation because you will walk ten miles a day and carry your own sleeping bag and food. The price includes airfare, food, tent and sleeping bag, and a travel guide for your two-week adventure. This tour is offered in the spring or fall only.

Vacation Number 3

On this vacation, you will enjoy the warm weather and meet the friendly people of Bali, Indonesia. While in Bali, you can relax on the beach. You can also learn about Balinese history, language, and culture. You can study art or dance with a local artist or you can learn how to cook Balinese food. On this trip, you will stay with a family in their home. One low price includes food and lodging. Airfare is extra. Travel in August or December.

4A. PRONUNCIATION

You can only go to the Ice Hotel in winter.

You can't go in summer.

A: Can I go snowshoeing near the hotel?

B: Yes, you can.

Exercise 1

1. Mr. Bay can—bacon: Mr. Bay can cook bacon.

2. Joe can—chicken: Joe can cook chicken.

3. Maxy can—Mexican: Maxy can cook Mexican food.

Exercise 2

Travel Agent: You can ski near the Ice Hotel.

Customer: Can you shop?

Travel Agent: No, you can't shop.

Exercise 3

1. You can't go ice fishing.

2. You can't go shopping.

3. You can visit an old church.

4. You can't go in the summer.

5. You can go to a museum.

6. You can go cross-country skiing.

UNIT 9: Staying Healthy

2A. LISTENING ONE: *Thin-Fast*

Man: So don't wait another minute. You should try Thin-Fast today. To order your Thin-Fast, call 1-800-555-THIN. That's 1-800-555-8446. Call today and get eight weeks of Thin-Fast for only $39.99. Yes, that's only $39.99 for the best weight-loss product money can buy. Call now and become happy, healthy, and thin!

Radio Announcer: This is WRAL radio. Now back to another forty minutes of continuous music . . .

LISTENING FOR MAIN IDEAS

Man: Are you overweight? Do you feel fat and unhealthy? Then you should try our amazing weight-loss remedy, Thin-Fast Diet Tea. Thin-Fast Diet Tea is a drink that will help you to lose weight fast. Here's one of our happy customers to tell you about it herself. Mary Ann, what do you think about Thin-Fast Diet Tea?

Mary Ann: Oh, it's terrific! It changed my life.

Man: Really? How did it change your life?

Mary Ann: Well, three months ago I was overweight and unhealthy. I ate fattening food and I never exercised. I looked terrible and I felt terrible. Before that, I had tried many different diets and weight-loss remedies, but nothing had worked. I just couldn't lose weight. I was so unhappy! Then one day I decided to try Thin-Fast Diet Tea. It really worked! With Thin-Fast, I lost sixty-five pounds in only three months. Now I'm thin and happy. I feel healthy and energetic, and everyone says I look great!

Man: I agree! You look terrific, Mary Ann. So tell us, how do you use Thin-Fast?

Mary Ann: Oh, it's very easy to use. You just drink one cup of Thin-Fast twice a day, once in the morning and once in the evening. That's all! And the best part is, you don't have to exercise, and you don't have to go on a diet.

Man: Really? That sounds too good to be true. So, how does Thin-Fast work?

Mary Ann: Well, Thin-Fast helps you to lose weight in two different ways. First, it stops you from feeling hungry. After drinking a cup of Thin-Fast, you don't feel hungry, so you will eat less food and lose weight.

Man: That's great. But with Thin-Fast do you have to stop eating fattening foods?

Mary Ann: Not at all! With Thin-Fast, you can eat all the fattening foods that you love, and you will never gain weight. You see, the second way that Thin-Fast works is that it prevents your body from taking in the calories from foods that make you gain weight. With Thin-Fast, I ate chocolate and ice cream every day, I never exercised, and I still lost weight.

Man: That's just amazing, Mary Ann. But is Thin-Fast a healthy way to lose weight?

Mary Ann: Oh, yes. It's very safe and healthy. It doesn't have any side effects at all. In fact, in China people have safely used the natural ingredients in Thin-Fast to lose weight for 2,000 years.

Man: Two thousand years?

Mary Ann: That's right. And today, people still use it to lose weight.

Man: So, what's it made of? What are the ingredients of Thin-Fast?

Mary Ann: It's made from 100 percent natural herbs. There's nothing artificial in Thin-Fast.

Man: That's great, but I know that losing weight can make you feel tired. How do you feel when you drink Thin-Fast? Do you feel tired?

Mary Ann: Oh, no. The natural herbs in Thin-Fast will help you to feel more energetic, so you will never feel tired or hungry.

Man: And how does Thin-Fast taste? Most diet drinks taste terrible.

Mary Ann: Oh, not Thin-Fast. It tastes great. It comes in two delicious flavors, orange and lemon. So losing weight is as easy as drinking a delicious cup of tea.

Man: That's wonderful, Mary Ann! Now I'm sure you'll agree that Thin-Fast is the fast and easy way to lose weight.

Mary Ann: That's right!

Man: So don't wait another minute. You should try Thin-Fast Diet Tea today. To order your Thin-Fast, call 1-800-555-THIN. That's 1-800-555-8446. Call today and get eight weeks of

Thin-Fast for only $39.99. Yes, that's only $39.99 for the best weight-loss product money can buy. Call now and become happy, healthy, and thin!

Radio Announcer: This is WRAL radio. Now back to another forty minutes of continuous music . . .

LISTENING FOR DETAILS

(Repeat Listening for Main Ideas.)

REACTING TO THE LISTENING

Excerpt One

Are you overweight? Do you feel fat and unhealthy? Then you should try our amazing weight-loss remedy, Thin-Fast Diet Tea.

Excerpt Two

Man: Here's one of our happy customers to tell you about it herself. Mary Ann, what do you think about Thin-Fast Diet Tea?

Mary Ann: Oh, it's terrific! It changed my life.

Excerpt Three

Mary Ann: It's made from 100 percent natural herbs. There's nothing artificial in Thin-Fast.

Excerpt Four

Mary Ann: With Thin-Fast, I ate chocolate and ice cream every day, I never exercised, and I still lost weight.

Man: That's just amazing, Mary Ann!

2B. LISTENING TWO: *Health Problems and Remedies*

Conversation One

Woman: Hi. How are you doing?

Man: Oh, not too well.

Woman: Really? What's the matter?

Man: Well, I have a bad stomachache. I think I ate too many chili peppers for lunch.

Woman: Oh, that's too bad. Maybe you shouldn't eat such spicy foods. Why don't you try drinking some peppermint tea?

Man: Peppermint tea?

Woman: Yes, peppermint tea is a natural herbal remedy for stomachaches. It really works!

Man: Thanks anyway, but I think I'll go to the drugstore and get some medicine.

Conversation Two

Woman: *(coughing and groaning)*

Man: Wow, you sound pretty sick. What's wrong?

Woman: Oh, I have a terrible cold. I keep getting a lot of colds and I don't know why.

Man: I'm sorry to hear that. Maybe you ought to take better care of yourself. I think you shouldn't work so hard.

Woman: Yeah, you're right. I do work a lot. But I can't quit my job. There must be something else I can do.

Man: Maybe you should try eating garlic. Garlic is really good for you. It can prevent you from catching so many colds. It really works for me. I take garlic every day, and I never get sick.

Woman: Garlic? But it's so bad for your breath!

Man: Not if you take garlic pills. There aren't any side effects with garlic pills.

Woman: Well, OK. I'll give it a try.

4A. PRONUNCIATION

I was overweight and unhealthy.

I wanted to lose weight. So, I decided to try Thin-Fast.

Thin-Fast is a safe and healthy way to lose weight.

I loved to eat fattening foods and I hated to exercise.

Some weight-loss products are made with artificial ingredients, but Thin-Fast is made with only natural ingredients.

I looked terrible and I felt terrible.

I just couldn't lose weight.

Exercise 2

1. Thin-Fast is amazing! It really works!

2. It's made from 100 percent natural herbs.

3. You just drink one cup of Thin-Fast twice a day.

4. You don't have to exercise, and you don't have to go on a diet.

5. You can eat fattening foods every day, and you'll never gain weight.

6. I lost sixty-five pounds in only three months.

7. Now I'm thin and happy.

Exercise 4

1. A: What kind of tea are you drinking?

   B: Thin-Fast tea.

2. A: Should I drink it three times a day?

   B: No, you should only drink it twice a day.

3. A: Which flavor do you prefer?

   B: I like the orange flavor.

   A: Really? I prefer the lemon flavor.

4. A: Garlic is really good for your health.

   B: Really? But garlic is so bad for your breath.

   A: Not if you take garlic pills.

5. A: These chili peppers are delicious. I love chili peppers.

   B: I like them too, but I can't eat them.
      They always give me a stomachache.

   A: Really? That's too bad. You could try drinking peppermint tea. It's very good for stomachaches.

UNIT 10: Endangered Languages

2A. LISTENING ONE: *Language Loss*

Professor: Good morning, class. Today, I'd like to talk about endangered and dead languages. So . . . What do you suppose a dead language is?

Student 1: Ummm . . . Is it a language that nobody speaks anymore, you know, like Latin?

Professor: Yes, that's it. Now, how about an endangered language? What's an endangered language?

LISTENING FOR MAIN IDEAS

Professor: Good morning, class. Today, I'd like to talk about endangered and dead languages. So . . . What do you suppose a dead language is?

Student 1: Ummm . . . Is it a language that nobody speaks anymore, you know, like Latin?

Professor: Yes, that's it. Now, how about an endangered language? What's an endangered language?

Student 1: Maybe it's a language that could die . . . Right?

Professor: Right. An endangered language is a language that could die, or become extinct soon. Most linguists agree there are over 6,000 languages in the world, and some linguists think that 90 percent could be endangered or dead by the year 2100.

Professor: Yes, that's a lot! Yes . . . You had a question.

Student 2: Why is it important? I mean, why do linguists care about dying languages? There are so many! Besides, doesn't everything die?

Professor: Well, yes, everything dies, but languages don't have to die. Besides, when a language dies, part of the culture can die too. Now this doesn't always happen. For instance, the Manx people on the Isle of Man in the Irish Sea have lost their native language, but they have kept their culture and traditions as Manx.

But think about what is expressed through language: Stories, ceremonies, poetry, humor, a whole way of thinking and feeling . . . When a language dies, all of this may be lost. So, culture is lost, too.

Also, history and knowledge are passed down through language, so when the language disappears, important information and knowledge may be lost, too.

So those are a few reasons why people care about language loss.

All right . . . Now, how do languages become endangered and extinct?

Student 3: Well, I guess nobody speaks them or studies them.

Professor: Yes. And this happens for several reasons. The government can make it illegal to teach the language in school. For example, before 1987, it was illegal to teach the Hawaiian language in Hawaii's public schools. It was difficult for children to learn the language. As a result, the language became endangered. Starting in 1987, programs teaching the Hawaiian language began. Today, there are approximately 2,000 students enrolled in these programs and more new programs are slowly opening.

In another situation, if one community has more power than another community, often the less powerful community feels it must learn the language of the more powerful group. Two things could happen in this situation. One, the language could be totally replaced. One example is the case of Native American languages spoken in what is now the United States. Once, there were hundreds of Native American languages. Now, more and more people speak English, and not the native languages. Children are not learning the languages, so when the last speaker dies, the languages will die too. If this continues, Native American languages will become extinct.

So, the language could be replaced. Or, the less powerful community could keep their native language and learn the other language too. An example of this is in Greenland where students learn Kalaallisut and Danish. They are bilingual; they learn both languages, so they won't lose their native language. This can help save endangered languages.

Student 2: So . . . Are people doing anything else to save the dying languages?

Professor: Yes, linguists are trying to save endangered languages. Linguists help create community programs where people can study the language so the language won't die. Also, they try to preserve as many endangered languages as they can. They make videotapes, audiotapes, and written records of language with translations. They also study the vocabulary and rules of the language and write dictionaries and grammar books.

OK, that's a lot of information for one lecture! We talked about endangered and dying languages, why it's important to save languages, how languages die, and how people can save endangered languages. Great! So for next time, please read the next chapter in the book.

LISTENING FOR DETAILS

(*Repeat Listening for Main Ideas.*)

REACTING TO THE LISTENING

Excerpt One

Student 2: Why is it important? I mean, why do linguists care about dying languages. There are so many! Besides, doesn't everything die?

Excerpt Two

Student 2: So . . . Are people doing anything else to save the dying languages?

2B. LISTENING TWO: *My Life, My Language*

Woman: I am Maori, living in New Zealand. In school, I learned and spoke English; it was the official language. Everything was taught in English in school. That was the government policy. I only heard Maori when I was with my grandparents. I could understand a little Maori, but could not speak it. I could not have a conversation with my grandparents because they did not speak English.

When I was in school, I knew that I was not learning the Maori culture, and I felt separated from my grandparents because of that. I felt empty inside and different from my family.

Maori is an endangered language and if children stop learning it, it will die. I do not want to see Maori disappear. So now that I am an adult and have children of my own, I decided I wanted my children to learn their native language. I found a pre-school that teaches children Maori before they enter school where they will learn English. The schools are called "language nests." In 1981, a group of Maori leaders saw that Maori was endangered and dying. They decided to do something. They did not want to wait for the government to do anything, so they got together and came up with the idea of pre-schools where children could learn Maori. Now, there are over 700 language nests and more than 13,000 children who are bilingual in Maori and English. Language nests are a big part of Maori education. Also in 1987, the government recognized Maori as the official language of New Zealand, with English too.

The children learn the basic values of the Maori culture. We have a strong belief in love, compassion, caring, hospitality, family responsibilities, and respect for elders. Children also learn our Maori stories. And through the language nests, children learn these values, as well as the language.

I also wanted to learn more about my language and culture. Now, there are classes for adults like me. The teachers are all older Maoris, usually grandparents. We meet in neighborhood centers. There are also week-long classes where adults can go and study. In these courses, no English is spoken all week!

Everything is Maori. The programs are good because now there are many more adults who speak Maori. It helps our children who are also learning Maori.

4A. PRONUNCIATION

When my children start school, they'll learn English.

My children won't forget Maori, because I'll speak it at home.

Nick'll give me a nickel.

"Whattul" you do?

Exercise 1

1. When I have children, I'll make sure they speak Maori.

2. When they go to school, they'll study only English.

3. If you go to Greenland, you'll hear two languages.

4. If the language dies, the culture won't survive.

5. In 2100, there won't be as many languages as now.

6. In the future, many children won't speak the same languages as their grandparents.

The Phonetic Alphabet

Consonant Symbols

/b/	**b**e		/t/	**t**o
/d/	**d**o		/v/	**v**an
/f/	**f**ather		/w/	**w**ill
/g/	**g**et		/y/	**y**es
/h/	**h**e		/z/	**z**oo, bu**s**y
/k/	**k**eep, **c**an		/θ/	**th**anks
/l/	**l**et		/ð/	**th**en
/m/	**m**ay		/ʃ/	**sh**e
/n/	**n**o		/ʒ/	vi**s**ion, A**s**ia
/p/	**p**en		/tʃ/	**ch**ild
/r/	**r**ain		/dʒ/	**j**oin
/s/	**s**o, **c**ircle		/ŋ/	lo**ng**

Vowel Symbols

/ɑ/	f**a**r, h**o**t		/iy/	w**e**, m**ea**n, f**ee**t
/ɛ/	m**e**t, s**ai**d		/ey/	d**ay**, l**a**te, r**ai**n
/ɔ/	t**a**ll, b**ou**ght		/ow/	g**o**, l**ow**, c**oa**t
/ə/	s**o**n, **u**nder		/uw/	t**oo**, bl**ue**
/æ/	c**a**t		/ay/	t**i**me, b**uy**
/ɪ/	sh**i**p		/aw/	h**ou**se, n**ow**
/ʊ/	g**oo**d, c**ou**ld, p**u**t		/oy/	b**oy**, c**oi**n

Credits

Reviewers

Lubie G. Alatriste, Lehman College; **A. Morgan Andaluz**, Leeward Community College; **Chris Antonellis**, Boston University CELOP; **Christine Baez**, Universidad de las Américas, Mexico City, Mexico; **Betty Baron**, Johnson County Community College; **Rudy Besikof**, University of California San Diego; **Mary Black**, Institute of North American Studies; **Dorothy Buroh**, University of California, San Diego; **Kay Caldwell**, Leeward Community College; **Margarita Canales**; Universidad Latinoamericana, Mexico City, Mexico; **Jose Carvalho**, University of Massachusetts Boston; **Philip R. Condorelli**, University of Massachusetts Boston; **Pamela Couch**, Boston University CELOP; **Barbara F. Dingee**, University of Massachusetts Boston; **Jeanne M. Dunnet**, Central Connecticut State University; **Samuela Eckstut-Didier**, Boston University CELOP; **Patricia Hedden**, Yonsei University; **Hostos Community College**; **GEOS Language Institute**; **Jennifer M. Gerrity**, University of Massachusetts Boston; **Lis Jenkinson**, Northern Virginia Community College; **Glenna Jennings**, University of California, San Diego; **Diana Jones**, Instituto Angloamericano, Mexico City, Mexico; **Matt Kaeiser**, Old Dominion University; **Regina Kandraska**, University of Massachusetts Boston; **King Fahd University of Petroleum & Minerals**; **Chris Ko**, Kyang Hee University; **Charalambos Kollias**, The Hellenic-American Union; **Barbara Kruchin**, Columbia University ALP; **Language Training Institute**; **Jacqueline LoConde**, Boston University CELOP; **Mary Lynch**, University of Massachusetts Boston; **Julia Paranionova**, Moscow State Pedagogical University; **Pasadena City College**; **Pontifical Xavier University**; **Natalya Morozova**, Moscow State Pedagogical University; **Mary Carole Ramiowski**, University of Seoul; **Jon Robinson**, University of Seoul; **Michael Sagliano**, Leeward Community College; **Janet Shanks**, Columbia University ALP; **Eric Tejeda**; PROULEX, Guadalajara, Mexico; **Truman College**; **United Arab Emirates University**; **University of Minnesota**; **Karen Whitlow**, Johnson County Community College

Notes

Notes

Notes